Praise for Jozanne Marie

"Jozanne Marie has demonstrated the high standards of excellence that Jamaica has come to expect from its sons and daughters. With her performance she has started a long overdue conversation on the Jamaican Diaspora in Canada. Jozanne is definitely one of Jamaica's most beautiful creations. We will be doing our part to keep this conversation active in the Diaspora and 'back a yard' when it comes to uplifting women."
—George Grant, Jamaican Consulate of Montreal

"*Beautiful* is a thought provoking story of hope. It is a great story on forgiveness, faith, and bravery despite unbelievable adversities. The play will empower women and change the lives of those who see it. It is *Beautiful*."
—Sheryl Lee Ralph, Award-Winning Actress

"*Beautiful* transforms family ugliness and breaks the cycle of violence. It is a true story of Courage and Victory."
—*OurWeekly* Magazine

"Jozanne has moved in places I have not visited in a long time. Everybody needs to hear this. She is anointed and her words are necessary."
—Legendary Roz Ryan

"*Beautiful* gives other women a voice to speak for themselves."
—Andrea Navedo, Award-Winning Actress (*Jane the Virgin*)

"Jozanne Marie's *Beautiful* is as emotionally powerful as it is inspirational. It's poignant and powerful. Ms. Marie is as gracious as she is talented."
—John Loprieno, Moorpark College

"It is rare that you see something this fantastic! Truly amazing! Pick of the week? Try pick of the year!"
—NAACP Board Member

"The honesty, the great story telling and the commitment. *Beautiful* was beautiful."
—Charlayne Woodard, Actress, Playwright, Award-Winning Actress

"Overall, *Beautiful* has an amazing dialogue, whimsical Jamaican connection; sensitive taboo subjects that make you face your own reflection. Jozanne's work is stunning, vibrant, and honest! Arise is another Ntozake Shange."
—DaMonique Ballou

"If, after sharing Marie's harrowing experiences and luminous catharsis, you still (like me) can't quite achieve her capacity for forgiveness, you will certainly be moved and inspired by it. *Beautiful* is stunning and courageous."
—Margaret Gray, *LA Times*

"*Beautiful* transforms family ugliness. Breaking the cycle of violence."
—William Clay Evans, *OurWeekly LA*

"It reminds students that they have the power to make change in their life, to confront issues that seem insurmountable and through the play's message, to find the courage to forgive, to heal, and to move on. As a personal memoir, *Beautiful* carries a strong lesson and I look forward to see how this will impact the campus community."
—Paula Crisostomo, Assistant Dean of Students for Intercultural Affairs, Occidental College

"*Beautiful* is a message of hope and inspiration for many women."
—H.E. Janice Miller, High Commissioner for Jamaica to Canada

BEAUTIFUL
UNASHAMED AND UNAFRAID

JOZANNE MARIE

Foreword by Kathy Ireland

A SAVIO REPUBLIC BOOK
An Imprint of Post Hill Press
ISBN: 978-1-64293-120-4
ISBN (eBook): 978-1-64293-121-1

Beautiful:
Unashamed and Unafraid
© 2019 by Jozanne Marie
All Rights Reserved

Cover Design by Tricia Principe, principedesign.com
Cover Photo by Brian Love Photography
Styling for the Cover Photo by Andrea Hall

posthillpress.com
New York • Nashville
Published in the United States of America

In Loving Memory of My Mother
Jean Maureen Ashley
*Thank you for being courageous when you were most afraid. You were
once silenced but today you will never be forgotten.
You are simply one of the bravest women I know.
Enjoy eternity.*

TABLE OF CONTENTS

Foreword 9

Introduction 11

Letter to You 18

Chapter 1: Home 21

Chapter 2: Mommy Dearest 40

Chapter 3: Don't Settle 57

Chapter 4: Playing on the Devil's Playground 68

Chapter 5: She Crazy 80

Chapter 6: Shameful Things 92

Chapter 7: No Gold Streets 108

Chapter 8: Secret Out 123

Chapter 9: When Daddies Go 135

Chapter 10: Touched by God 150

Chapter 11: Bye Saint Ann 158

Chapter 12: A Child Lost 167

Chapter 13: Runaway 176

Chapter 14: No More Secrets 187

Chapter 15: Returning to Love 200

Chapter 16: God Is Enough 209

Chapter 17: Life After Abuse 220

Chapter 18: Knights and Princesses 231

Chapter 19: A Vertical Leap 242

A Prayer for You 249

Declaration of Bravery 250

Join the Campaign 252

A Special Thank You 253

About the Author 256

FOREWORD

BEAUTIFUL IS A compelling, uplifting true story of triumph over trauma. How do we learn to forgive the most intimate and disturbing violations and abuses of body and spirit, by the very people we are told to trust completely? My friend, Jozanne Marie, is a brilliant artist, actor, author, and poet whose theatrical presentations of the story in these pages brings tears, laughter, love, and a testimony of the saving grace of faith that literally restored the tender heart of someone who is truly *Beautiful* in every conceivable way. Jozanne has opened her heart and very private life to share a story that is frighteningly more common than most of us would ever believe, in numbers that are staggering.

How does anyone who is a survivor of such horrific treatment and cruelty learn to trust, love, and find the grace and beauty that is a natural gift to every girl and woman? For Jozanne, who is my sister in Jesus Christ, faith is the shining light that rescued a soul which had been lied to, beaten, raped, and forced to have an abortion that Jozanne didn't want to have. To live through these agonies and find healing for all involved, including the very predator who was responsible for your protection, seems nearly impossible. Taking this journey with Jozanne and learning from her will empower your life and give you strength you didn't know you had.

In the very busy times that we live in today, asking anyone to read a book is a significant commitment. Your time and resources are excellent investments when you choose to read *Beautiful.* In the midst of unspeakable pain, tears, and loss, Jozanne reveals her own mistakes with stunning clarity. After years of suffering, it would be easy to gloss over Jozanne's own stumbles. This does not happen. Jozanne teaches us that a part of being *Beautiful* is living in harmony with God's word and facing our own participation in the mistakes of our lives.

BEAUTIFUL

Having worked in the fashion industry for decades, "beautiful" was always an unsettling word. It seemed to apply strictly to certain groups of people. That was offensive. The *Beautiful* found in this wonderful book is available to everyone. When Jozanne offered me the opportunity to write this foreword, it was intimidating. The book is so powerful and beautifully written that it was challenging to understand how to make a contribution to something that is so magnificent.

When speaking with Jozanne and loved ones, the reminder was to simply share the truth of the book's impact on my life and the lives of loved ones. Sadly, there are people in our lives who have suffered abuse and sexualization at unbelievably early years. Too often this pain sets a path for the abused to become an abuser. *In Beautiful* we travel the road Jozanne has taken while being concerned and alert to the choices that are all too frequent for survivors of PTSD.

Please purchase and read *Beautiful.* It is a powerful gift of recovery. The battle from broken to *Beautiful* must be shared. In our lives, we all know people who are hurting and seeking to live their lives in less pain. *Beautiful* is a wonderful answer to the questions, "How will I get better?" "Must my past be my present and my future?" "I believe in God and still my wounds are ever present." I love *Beautiful* because it answers these questions and so many more. Please share this book with your own heart and the heart and souls of people you know who must be reminded that no matter their past, their age, the color of their skin, or their weight, in the eyes of God, every single human life is *Beautiful* beyond words.

Kathy Ireland
Chair and CEO, Kathy Ireland Worldwide

INTRODUCTION

AFTER THE COMPLETION of my solo play, *Beautiful*, in 2013, I took the bold step to present it as a stage reading at the Los Angeles Theatre Center. With only fifteen people sitting in the audience and the lights glaring into my eyes, my heart pounded with anticipation and anxiety as to whether or not I could trust my audience to be sensitive with the raw details of my life.

It was time to share some intimate information that had brought me so much shame for several years. A burst of sweat hit the side of my face and the awkward stares mixed with silence made me a bit uncomfortable.

Uncertain if my audience would receive my message, I quietly prayed in my heart and quickly turned the pages to Act One. A few audience members were close friends and some were acquaintances, but the majority only knew me as a strong and confident woman rather than a once broken and lost girl. These people were never a witness to the flames that burned in my soul and I am sure it surprised them that at one time I smelled like the fragrance of death.

That Friday evening, it was my time to step into the light and reveal the darkness in which I once abided. Life had come full circle and I finally had the courage to face my deepest fears. It was time to let go of the girl I once knew. My inner child was ready to speak. She no longer wanted to conceal all that she was ashamed of. She was all grown up, ready to face her enemies—and most of all the demons—that kept her chained to fear and doubt. Although she had developed some amazing friendships, the silence of her past still made them strangers.

At the time of the stage reading I was uncertain why it was imperative to disclose my life in such a transpicuous way, but deep inside my heart, I knew the moment was now.

BEAUTIFUL

For ninety minutes I read my script, danced, and cried in front of a taken-aback audience. I had become the narrator of my past, and looking from the outside of my experiences, it was as if I was talking about someone else's life. The old me was emotional, reckless, and had no boundaries. But this girl I have grown to love had become sober, wise, and free. She was beautiful, not just physically, but had earned her stripes in maturity. Anything that was an obstacle to my soul thriving in God had to go. The people who had failed me in my childhood were no longer giants, but mere characters of a story I no longer was a part of.

The reproach had slipped away like a forgotten memory and the secret I once feared being exposed was now my redemption. Purpose was birthed. I was standing in the midst of destiny and it was clear to me that God's plan for my life was much bigger than what I had suffered.

The audience cheered and cried, and some sat speechless at the fact that I went through so many tragic ordeals. To some, it was quite shocking to witness the cheery, strong, and playful woman they knew was once unhappy, fragile, and grave. When the stage reading came to a close, their hugs spoke volume and their smiles welcomed me home to myself. That night I walked away like one of God's mighty men, David. My little stone had hit Goliath straight between the eyes and the shame of my past came tumbling down.

It was the same night actor; Geoff Rivas came on as a director. Within a year, *Beautiful*, the solo play, had its world premiere at the Los Angeles Theatre Center produced by the Latino Theater Company.

For five weeks, four days a week, I bared my soul to complete strangers about the issues of abuse, the effects it had on my life, and how I conquered the beast. Following my four weeks' run, *Beautiful*, garnered an LA Times Critics' Choice Award and an NAACP Theatre Award for Best Solo Play. Since then I have been touring different colleges, churches, and theaters presenting *Beautiful* and its message of hope, forgiveness, and healing. The title was inspired

INTRODUCTION

from Ecclesiastes 3:11 where it says, "God has made everything beautiful in its time." Beautiful, a word convoluted by magazine covers, TV commercials, billboard ads, and current trends. At first I did not know what I was embarking on when I chose the word "beautiful," but soon it would become clear that beauty was way more than how we physically looked, but the disposition of our hearts.

Yes, God was dispelling the darkness with his marvelous light. Not only did my life transform, but my audience experienced their own freedom. The most fulfilling element during the tour was chatting with hundreds of individuals who privately pulled me aside after each show and shared their own secrets with me. It stirred my heart and reminded me once again of God's love and His grace for mankind.

I can never forget the night when a Jewish woman in her late seventies waited patiently to the side while I shook the hands of each guest. Just a few inches away, her teary and aged eyes drew my curiosity. It was obvious she had a story to tell. Her body shook and tears rolled down her face as I walked towards her. When I got closer, she grabbed onto my hand, looked me into my eyes, but no words came out of her mouth. For a moment I thought she was mute, but eventually she said, "Young lady, thank you so much for doing this play. I am a survivor of rape and for the first time in my life, I feel beautiful tonight."

Speechless and emotional, we held onto each other like two lost sisters who had reunited. There was an unspoken language between us that we had not only survived, but we had conquered the cultural silence to protect and not expose when sexually violated. She was free of her vocal quiescence, and we celebrated with tears of joy and the longest embrace.

On another occasion, a stunning redhead shared her experience of being gang raped the beginning of that year. Although she disclosed this tragedy with family members, it was her first time revealing this information to a stranger. Her chest caved in as she relived that horrible night when three men spiked her drink, and she found herself naked on their bathroom floor the following morning. She, too, was ready to take her freedom and her voice back.

Another night in Atlanta following the show, a woman stood up and shared about being raped at the age of eight by her mother's trusted friend. She hadn't the courage to unveil this secret to her mother until her perpetrator died. By then she was fifty years old. She shared how she once weighed 289 pounds, and it was not until she revealed the secret to her mother that she lost eighty-five pounds within four months. These are only a few of the stories out of the hundreds I have heard.

It was like electricity moved though the audience as one by one strangers popped out of their seats to win the war against cultural silence and shame. No one was eager to go home. We all needed to continue the conversation. The play was stirring hearts, bringing healing and hope to those who had lost sight of the truth that they were worthy of restoration. Burdens were lifted, confusion cleared, and freedom restored.

However, it was mindboggling to me as to why it took such a lengthy time for the victims of sexual assault to share these issues. I could not comprehend why these heinous crimes were kept secret at the spiritual detriment of one's own soul—and sometimes physical life—for such a lengthy time. Finally it dawned on me that people were not keeping secrets; people were preventing ridicule and shame.

The common denominator in every story was the humiliation and degradation everyone felt at one point or another and the fear to confront it. As someone who was once violated sexually, I too have experienced the thief in the night and was too afraid to scream for help. We all sat and watched our virtue be hijacked and stolen. The shame of our past was burdensome and we needed it not only lifted, but forgotten. We wanted our purity and innocence back.

There was a need for men and women everywhere to discover liberty and hear the sound of their authentic voices again. It wasn't just their voices silenced; it seemed as if God was silent as well. But was God silent or were we not listening? Although I had taken my leap of faith, this matter was bigger than me. It was a universal stage with hundreds of stories ready to exhale; the shame does not belong to me. It was time to leave the shame behind, come out of hiding, and embrace the truth that we are all fearfully and wonderfully made by an awesome God who knows how to redeem the ruined places of our lives.

That night after speaking to the Jewish woman, her teary eyes told me this was more than a play. The truth was being sent forth to set captives free and I was its first candidate. It was necessary to keep the conversation going. It was clear to me that my experience came with the responsibility to join the rest of freedom fighters to win the war against the cultural silence of sexual abuse victims. Yet this fight seemed enormous. I had no clue where to begin. There were too many obstacles to overcome and questions I wasn't sure I had the answer to. The majority of people I came across were either too afraid or too ashamed to talk about it.

Where was I going to begin, with few resources and limited contacts? How was I going to make a difference in the lives of women across the world that even feared for their own lives if they dared to expose the secrets they held? What would happen if I went down this road? While I wasn't sure, I simply knew it was the right thing to do. The great British philosopher, political economist, and civil servant John Stuart Mill said, "Bad men need nothing more to compass their ends, than that good men should look on and do nothing."

Like Moses had a staff, I had a pen and paper; well, a laptop and a testimony. It was time to sound the alarm and wake up those who had been forgotten in the shadows of a sexual catastrophe. It was time to ring the freedom bells for the daughters and sons to no longer be tossed to the winds of regret and brokenness. God wanted to show us He is the repairer of broken walls. Yes, it was the time for self-discovery and restoration for men and women who had lost their identities in a sea of sexual violence. The weed and tares of our past have stifled virtue and identity for too long. This was the time God not only wanted to restore shattered dreams, but rebuild broken lives and repair our flawed self-images.

I felt the Spirit of God saying, "You are my daughter; give me your hand and let me dance with you." It was God's breath blowing into our souls once again to breathe life and recover a new identity. But it was not going to happen without a fight. The invisible tape placed on the mouths of women around the world by those who intimidated them with coercion, threats, and manipulation needed to be removed. This fight demanded not only legislation passed, it also required us to be brave enough to say, "No more secrets." We had to be relentless, unashamed and unafraid.

Those who were abused and taken advantage of needed to be reminded that they were made in the image of God: pure, holy, and beautiful. It was going to take us being courageous to believe the truth and choose the life that was intended for us before the foundations of the world.

Beautiful is about saying no to the secrets we have held on to and letting go of the shame they have caused. It is about baring the truth with a reckless abandon at our own pace. It is that moment in time when we resolve:

"I don't belong here."

"This is not who I am."

"I will no longer carry the degradation of the person who hurt me."

"I will not backpack the scars they left through my journey."

And, "I will not let their definition of me be my anthem, nor will I allow their depraved decisions control my destiny."

When reading Ecclesiastes 3:11, part of the verse states, "*He has made everything beautiful in his time.*" I often wondered what that verse means. Could it be possible that *in its time* means a place of maturity? We oftentimes look at something or someone and say, it's beautiful. But what makes it beautiful? Oftentimes, when we describe something as beautiful, we become fascinated and captivated by the details. And behind that detail, we can't ignore it took time, energy, and thought. The encounter with beauty is an experience and most times we don't forget it.

What if what this *"beautiful in his time"* God is talking about is more than our outer appearance and more of an internal awakening of our soul, where we discover the truth of who we are and why we are here? That to comprehend beauty and walk in the place of "beautiful" is to get to the nitty-gritty of why the breath of life exists in our bodies right now and to be courageous to live out the purpose of God, despite the tragedy we face. It is simply remembering the authenticity of our individual voices that so often get shut out by the tragedies we experience. "Beautiful "says, "I am who God says I am. I no longer need to be understood, but to understand the bigger picture of my existence in this world I have been thrown in and to fulfill the destiny I have been assigned. I have matured. I am awake. I am born again in my soul. I am beautiful.

In conclusion, here is my truth and why I decided to be unafraid and unashamed. I pray my story, self- discovery, and revelations will not only inspire you, but motivate you to live again, breathe again, and find your "beautiful" again.

Dedicated to you, brave and beautiful one.

JOZANNE MARIE

LETTER TO YOU

Dear Beautiful,

I always find myself a little nervous to confront or even talk about abuse. Fear. Terror. Shame. Guilt. These feelings are normal reactions for anyone who has been abused. But today, I challenge you to change that. I petition you to receive love, be courageous, embrace your truth, and release shame. For it is when we confront our biggest fears we experience our greatest freedom.

It's time to leave the past behind and begin a new chapter. "Forgetting what is behind and reaching forward to what is ahead." Philippians 3:13. Let today be your day of resurrection. Let it be the brightest day you ever set your eyes upon, because you have resolved to confront your fears and recognize your worth. Be free like a bird, uninhibited by the winds of change. Be no longer comfortable with pain, oppression, and self-loathing. In the pages hereafter I will share the depths of my heart to remind you that you are not alone on the quest for virtue, beauty, and truth.

Understand that some days the sun will shine perfectly, and other days the gloom of your past will spread across your mind like a cloudy day. You probably feel like kicking yourself for going back to this dark place after telling yourself countless times, "I will leave the past behind me." But keep in mind, sometimes it's difficult to let go of justice when it's denied. Pursue your freedom. It's your birthright.

I myself have travelled down that road of regret, uncertainty, and sorrow countless times due to being molested as a child. Sometimes we feel like we have travelled so far away from the truth we can't get back to the people we were. There are way too many secrets, too much brokenness and silence to become whole again. Instead we dwell on the past and eventually become comfortable in the ruined places.

We often believe if we hold onto our silence a tad bit longer, in some way we will discover ourselves again without going through the agony of uncloaking the secrets that left us handicapped. Yet to conceal a secret is like walking around with an inferno, and we fear if we release it, it will unleash like venom and everyone will get hurt. Soon enough we are set aflame by the poison it creates inside us and gradually we don't remember who we are and what we even sound like.

Beautiful one, you are not alone. May these following pages be a mirror in which you see yourself and a transparent voice of everything you wanted to say but never quite got around to it.

It is those things in our lives we are most ashamed and afraid of that distort our perception of ourselves. It makes it absolutely difficult to believe we are beautiful in the sight of God and others. It creates a crooked path that navigates us to dead ends and ultimately takes us into captivity. However, life does not have to remain the way it is; it can change and will change when we make a choice to change. In some divine way regardless of or differences and belief may we be able to connect with each other through these pages, and as a result some light be shed that will grant clarity, healing, and restoration.

With you all the way,
Jozanne Marie

CHAPTER 1

HOME

THE SKATEBOARDERS, SURFERS, and blondes in bikinis living in Hermosa Beach, California, still can't erase the memory of that orange house up the street in Rolling Town, Kingston, Jamaica. 29 Milk Avenue was where my training began. God was preparing my heart for war and my mind for battle. Those two rooms we occupied were the battlefield I was born into and my escape out of the trenches of Kingston, Jamaica left me with two choices. I was either going to be a casualty of war or discover that the home and family I was born into had nothing to do with my identity.

There was an omnipotent God who had a plan for my life. "*Not a plan to destroy me but a future and a hope.*" Jeremiah 29:11. My home experience or where I was born was irrelevant. With a deeper revelation about who I am, the outcome of my life in this world had to do with two things—*choice and faith.*

As a poor black Caribbean girl, how I showed up in the world depended on the choices I was going to make and what I believed about myself, despite my tumultuous past and all the obstacles in the world that did not favor my success. After the age of six, living in a huge house with both biological parents and a white picket fence like the one on *Little House on the Prairie* became the dream. I wanted my family to be just like the Brady Bunch. Mom. Dad. Brothers. Sisters. Love. Family. We would sit around the Thanksgiving table just like the Huxtables' where aunties and uncles would come over and tell stories about what life was like when they were young.

BEAUTIFUL

That was how I imagined the perfect family to be. But unlike other little girls in our town, my household was different. I called my grandmother Mummy and the man she lived with Smith. All I knew of my biological mother was she needed to stay in the hospital due to her illness, which my grandparents felt uncomfortable about sharing at the time. My dad, well, he lived in the United States where the streets were paved with gold and you could buy anything you wanted for ninety-nine cents. Yes, that was what we were told about America. I must say, the ninety-nine cent stores are still one of my favorite places to shop. No shame about it.

Nevertheless, the insecurity and shortcomings of being in a disjointed family never began until I turned six years old. This was when I met my father and mother for the first time. Meeting them became the turning point in my life, one that would eventually define love, home, and identity for the next seventeen years. Before then, I was joyous, full of life, and uninhibited.

Do you remember what home was like for you as a child? How does it make you feel when you remember it? Is the home you were born into a huge part of why you have become the person you are today? Who were you as a child? Who are you now?

The reason I am asking all these questions is because as we get older we change and sometimes that change is not always due to age. Sometimes we change and become people we never planned on being due to childhood pain, shame, and rejection. I remember distinctly at the age of twenty-three when I looked into the mirror and did not recognize myself. I had turned into this suicidal, angry, and dark woman, far from the playful, imaginative, and free child I was growing up.

Everything was attainable at 29 Milk Avenue. Our orange house stuck between the suburbs and the ghetto was home. We rarely flinched at the gunshots we heard between the gang rivals due to the political tension between the People's National Party and the Jamaican

Labor Party. It was just another normal day and as long as we kept our political views to ourselves, the gangs left us alone.

It was just the three of us: Mummy, Smith, and me. We lived in two rooms rented from this lanky woman Ms. Cora who only came out of her house to collect the rent. At night all three of us slept on the same king sized Sealy bed. Opposite from our bed was an old English dresser we shared, filled with our clothes and valuables, like fake pearls, pendants, birth certificates, and letters from my dad in America. I slept in the corner, Mummy in the middle, and Smith snored the night away at the edge of the bed. Our bedroom and dining room was in the same space while our kitchen was just a few feet away from the bathroom. But no matter how congested our abode, this was our home, and trust me, there was never a dull moment in it.

Tony Tribe and UB40's "Red Red Wine" was a broken record in our house. Whenever one of their songs played, Mummy ran over to the radio, turned the volume up and said, "Come Jozanne, dance with me nu." Smith would sprawl back in his blue wooden chair, smoking a Craven A cigarette and sipping on a little red wine.

"Dance? Dancing wasn't meant for you people, man," he mock.

"Don't pay him any mind Jozanne. Child, don't let anyone take the dance out of your life. Life was meant to dance to." Mummy was a woman of vigor, strength, and sass.

MY GRANDMOTHER

My fair skinned lady danced to the sound of music.

Her own grooves.

Her own moves.

Her own tune.

There she lived in each frequency.

There she lived in each molecule.

She was a star.

BEAUTIFUL

My fair skinned lady danced to the sound of music

Her own grooves.

Her own moves.

Her own tune.

Each moment in her world was like the grass, waiting for the rain to come.

Sometimes the scorching sun dried up her smile.

But the sweetness of dried cocoa pods, ackee and salt-fish set the tone for the morning.

My fair skinned lady danced to the sound of music

Her own grooves.

Her own moves.

Her own tune.

Fried fish and bammy.

Scotch bonnet pepper.

Real ginger beer so strong you can sip it like a glass of cognac.

Bob Marley.

Marcia Griffith.

Ken Boothe.

My fair skinned lady danced to the sound of music.

Her own grooves.

Her own moves.

Her own tune.

UB-40 sparked many conversations.

Braids with beads synchronizing to each bop.

HOME

My fair skinned lady danced to the sound of music.
Her own grooves.
Her own moves.
Her own tune.

It was as if Mummy was teleported to another country. Each lyric had its own memory and she made sure to tell us the story behind every song, even if we'd heard it a million times. That day Smith was not going to steal her joy. We danced and danced until we ran out of breath. For a moment, her passion was overwhelming and intoxicating. Whatever Mummy did or said was done with devotion and affection. She was zealous, and bold as a lion.

One evening after school we were sitting on the steps of the verandah. Upset about my failing grade in art class, Mummy asked, "Did you think you deserved to pass?"

I didn't have an answer because I knew I did not give it my all.

"Anything you are going to do, do it with excellence," Mummy counseled me. "What you holding back for? Do you think God held back when he made the sun, the moon, and the world we live in? Passion created the world. Passion created you and me. Everything you do, do it with passion, Jozanne."

Mummy was filled with such wisdom. From that day, I set out to thrive for the best. We were like two peas in a pod. Mummy was my best friend. Wherever she went, I was always a step behind. It did not bother me that she was not my biological mother because she was all I knew. Mummy was just enough.

29 Milk Avenue was where I had my first love encounter. One night while Smith worked overnight at the airport I had a sudden case of food poisoning. A rash appeared on my face and spread, and everything I ate I hurled into the toilet. Since we did not own a phone, Mummy wasted no time. She quickly dressed me at 4 am, threw me over her shoulder, and carried me to the nearby hospital, which was a

mile away from where we lived. "Jesus help my baby," she prayed in a whisper.

This Jesus person was mentioned daily in our house right before the rooster crowed at 5:00 in the morning and right before bedtime. First, Mummy prayed and I followed with my own prayer written by Methodist Evangelist Charles Wesley in the 1700s: "Gentle Jesus, meek and mild, look upon this little child. Savior makes me what thou art, come and live within my heart." Saying that prayer every night and attending Maranatha Christian Church on Sundays was our tradition. As a child, Jesus was that big guy in the sky, looking at my every move. He was capable of making wrong things right, and just like Santa, He would only give us what we wanted if were nice. One day I was going to learn that I needed Jesus to be more than a tradition, I needed Jesus to be real to me.

Sometimes after prayer I asked Mummy, "Why am I always talking to God and He never talks back?" She replied, "He loves to listen more than He speaks. Just believe that He hears you."

"But how do I know what He wants if He does not speak?"

"Just listen, Jozanne."

"I don't hear anything, only the crickets outside."

"He is in your heart. Listen to your heart."

At the time none of that made any sense. My heart wanted all kind of things, like ice cream, mangoes, and playing dandy shandy with kids down the block.

Outside of Sunday school, most of my time learning about Jesus was on the steps of our front porch. "Come, let's catch the breeze," Mummy would beckon every evening after dinner. We would sit there and chat until the streetlights came on, which was the time I went to bed. On those steps Mummy consistently engrained in me that I was God's child.

"Royalty runs through our veins, Jozanne," she would always say. But I never thought we were royalty. Our two rooms were nothing like Buckingham Palace where Princess Diana lived.

I would tell her, "Mummy, we are not rich."

"Royalty has nothing to do with money. People can have millions, but are poor on the inside. Remember that."

These kinds of conversations between us gave me hope despite the fact we did not have much. No, we were not wealthy, but we believed princesses could live in the ghetto and my grandmother made sure to remind me every so often that I was one. When I climbed the mango tree in my skirt and threw stones at the little boys who said mean things to me after school, she reminded me, "You are a princess, don't let no one get you out of character." Yet I also believed princesses didn't have to be dainty and passive.

As a child I was always the awkward girl that never really fit in. It wasn't that people never liked me; I just thought outside the box, which most times made people uncomfortable. Back then in our town, tradition was more important than free thinking. Whether or not what we believed was working, crossing the cultural boundaries meant you were a rebel and had no loyalty to your people. For instance, the women in our culture needed to cook for their man. She was to be subservient to him, even if he was abusive. As long as he paid the bills, they kept silent about the abuse. I thought differently.

I needed to speak. I needed to know why everything was everything. The world had questions and God had the answers. Although I was determined to know the truth, Mummy was somewhat overprotective. Sometimes she chained the gate with a padlock so I could not go roaming the streets, but I just climbed over it. I needed to explore. I wanted to know the kids in my neighborhood, why Mr. Chin next door only came out of his house at 3:00 p.m., and why Ms. Cora, the landlady, never invited us into her house. If I could not escape the confinement of my house, I got creative, like building my own toys. Whatever came to mind, I was going to do it despite the opinions of others.

One day on our way home from the market, there was an old wheel left on the side of the road. I picked it up and asked Smith to attach a three-foot iron bar into it. I wanted to build a one-wheel cart. Smith laughed, "Carts don't have one wheel, Jozanne." I had a vision though. Despite that, I was determined we were going to make that cart. After much begging and pleading, Smith attached that wheel to the piece of iron bar and tied a box to it. For six years I ran around the yard at high speed with that cart as if it was the best invention in the world. I guess I always had a thing for old broken items and making use of them.

Everything in life was possible at age four. I felt invincible like Wonder Woman, and had a desire to help anyone who had fallen prey to the "bad guys" at school. Although Mummy thought I was too tomboyish at times, she was the one who told me I could be anything in this world. She affirmed my black skin, keeping it acne free by giving me the nectar from aloe vera plants to eat. I adored the rich texture of my hair except for when I had it washed with Palmolive soap and had to sit in the blazing sun for an hour for it to dry. My strands shriveled up like bacon and it took a lifetime to remove all the knots and kinks.

The neighbors heard me hollering miles away, as if I was being tortured. After that Mummy oiled my hair with Vaseline and made Bantu knots to hold in the moisture. "This is the Cleopatra beauty treatment," Mummy would say. Well I came to find out Cleopatra soaked her body in almond oils and bathed in milk and honey. As far as her hair, she soaked it with honey and castor oil. Apparently someone was not telling the truth.

Nevertheless, at no point did I ever equate "ugly" and "me" in the same sentence. Mummy affirmed my existence in the world by all the beauty treatments and the constant reminder that, "Nothing God created is ugly. Everything alive has a purpose."

Her affirmation granted me permission to have a mind of my own and not to be fearful of letting anyone knowing what was on it. Some thoughts were childish, like, "Why does the moon follow me wherever I go?" And others were more mature like "Why does a 'Good

God,' allow bad things to happen in a world He loves?" The idea of living on Earth just to make it to Heaven seemed ludicrous, even as a child. In the evening from my verandah, I prayed for Heaven to penetrate Earth because it was the current space in the universe I occupied.

God letting me dance with the moon and touch the stars with my fingertips was the beating of my heart. From my verandah steps the night sky stood glorious and I longed to discover it. Someone made those stars spark and the moon one huge light bulb in the sky. The same God who made those stars took the time to knit us together in our mother's womb. We too were meant to shine just like the Heavenly host above.

As a child, the neighbors considered me an old soul, and rightfully so. I was the only child living on the compound, surrounded by adults. As a result, I was left to my own thoughts and the adults who came over to visit. Sitting amongst the older women and hearing all their dirty secrets and gossip was way more entertaining and definitely matured me faster.

Sometimes Mummy would say, "Jozanne, don't you want go and play with something?" No, I wanted to know why Desmond did not come home last night, why Smith gets drunk all the time, and why Ingrid got rid of her baby without her husband knowing. This gathering was way more fascinating than playing hopscotch.

Whenever I was shunned away from the juicy details of their conversation, I ran around the yard with my one wheel cart or found a piece of stick to throw. Mummy thought I was reckless for a girl and many evenings she preached about modesty and being dainty. Although she wanted me to be a free thinker, in some way she had her own views about womanhood. It was fine for a woman to be intelligent and a hard worker, but she should always stifle any aggression that made her seem masculine. If she didn't she would never be married or be liked.

"Be gentle, Jozanne. You are a girl." She hated when I climbed the mango tree. "Girls don't climb trees." To me, the only difference between a girl and a boy was our private parts, and my private part was just fine climbing trees, racing boys down the street, and challenging any knucklehead to a fight. Although I reveled in my tomboy attitude during the week, I didn't mind being the princess on Sunday morning when I got dressed for church. A girl can do both. The freedom I felt as a child was how I thought God intended us to live, uninhibited, brave, and filled with love. Childhood was a time to explore, seek out the unknown, and discover the world.

At four years old, everything in my mind was grandiose and filled with color, but like I said earlier, everything changed when I was six. I came to realize that the wars affecting me had nothing to do with the slums we lived in but the brokenness inside of our own house.

Sometimes on those steps, besides sharing about God, Mummy compared Smith to Colin Thomas, the love of her life. She went and on about how great of a man he was and how much he loved my mother. Respect was important to her. "It does not matter if a man takes you around the world or buy you nice things. If he does not respect you, that man doesn't love you the way God intended a woman to be loved."

Mummy and Smith had an usual way of expressing love to each other. Smith frequently drank himself into a stupor and it made him lash out at Mummy. After a gruesome quarrel, out of embarrassment, Mummy hid herself in the house for a couple of days because she knew the neighbors heard how Smith degraded her.

Needless to say, at four years old I learned a lot about women, their men, and their need to be loved. 29 Milk Avenue was a house of deep secrets. I learned how easy it was for a woman to live with a man and not love him one inch. Sex and money was not enough, but admiration and tenderness carried great value. A woman needed to know she was not an overlooked pebble, but a sought after ruby. A man's love had to be way deeper than the wrestling between sheets and bringing home the bacon. A woman needed to know she was not only in his arms, but in his heart. His heart needed to be undivided while she was in it, and his presence welcoming at the sound her voice.

It was on those steps I learned a woman was capable of carrying the world on her shoulders while sporting a crown on her head. I felt Mummy's heaviness from the silent rejection of the man she submitted herself to, yet each day, her role-play of housewife took her further away from the truth that she was God's beloved. She too was royalty and beautiful.

It was obvious that things weren't fine and slowly I felt ashamed of where I lived. I wanted that white picket fence and the streets of gold, and the only way to attain that goal was to live with my father, Henry McPherson, in America. He moved there when I turned one. Every letter he wrote me was neatly folded and tucked under my clothes in the dresser drawer where we kept the fancy stuff. A night did not pass without me reading Dad's letters under the lantern next to the bed. I stared at the only photograph I had of him in his cream suit and a huge Afro, daydreaming of the day we would meet face to face. He had the keys to the golden city and I couldn't wait until the day he returned and swept me off my feet.

On the contrary, Mummy's main concern was making sure my father sent money to give me a decent education and a good meal each day. We didn't know when or if he would return to Jamaica, and until then we needed to manage under the dysfunctional living conditions with Smith.

Experiencing these things as a child, I vowed to never follow in Mummy's footsteps. Helplessness grieved my spirit and the thought of a woman in the arms of a man that made her feel inadequate, unappreciated, and depreciated did not make any lick of sense to me. Why would a woman stay in a place with anyone who did not enjoy her dance or make her laugh until she cracked a rib?

Not to mention Pastor Tony at Maranatha Church preached every Sunday that "God is good," "God is love," and God wanted the best for us. *"Yes Jesus loves me, this I know,"* was the theme song. Sunday after Sunday I tried wrapping my brain around Mummy's decision to live with a man who didn't love her.

Our lives did not reflect what we thought about ourselves or what we believed about God. Mummy was jobless, a single parent with a sick daughter, and now a granddaughter with absent parents. Smith was her lifeline, and like some women do in order to have financial security, she settled for the help.

But with Smith's money also came pain. The longer she stayed with him, the dimmer Mummy's light became. She vanished whenever he walked into the room. It was as if she believed it was her fault that Smith threw demeaning words like rocks across the dinner table as he ate the meal she prepared. She did everything to earn his love, but understand, love is like water, it flows freely from its cistern. No one can take credit for its origin. It's either there or it is not.

A beautiful, vibrant woman's spirit was crushed every time her man's ego got in the way. Smith knew the right button to push. Like a puppet on a string, he knew how to make her shrink, and at the same time manipulate her emotions with false promises to have her dancing again.

The dynamic of their relationship taught me one thing: to distrust any man. No one knew about this abusive relationship except the neighbors. Her only explanation for staying with him was "love people no matter what they have done." While love was her excuse for abuse, nothing could be further from the truth. This kind of love was different compared to the night she carried me on her shoulders to the hospital. Their "love" was filled with turmoil, confusion, and regrets. Her acceptance of abuse taught me that love was painful, complicated, and dramatic. And it was going to take my own toxic journey with false love to unlearn my grandparents' example. Speaker and author Devi Titus says, *"The home is the basis of all human society."* Whatever example we witness in our homes, as children we will carry on its legacy into our own lives.

HOME

It is never what parents say; it is always what they do that echoes most with children. My grandmother's passive and silent voice when taken advantage of subconsciously taught me abuse was acceptable. I needed to love people regardless if they were rude, untrustworthy, or volatile.

I learned in my home that it was acceptable for love to be toxic, and I learned how to keep the things that were hurtful and shameful a secret. "Keep your mouth closed, Jozanne, and don't let people in your business," she warned me. Our business did not belong anywhere in the streets. We were to pretend that all was well when the neighbors came over.

The longer the abuse took place, the less she accepted my free-spirited and opinionated ways. "Children are to be seen and not heard," she scolded me. I did not understand why it was wrong to stand up for myself, but as children we tend to believe anything our parents tell us. How frequently do we hear adults reprimanding children about knowing their place of silence? Yet when children are silenced by the things that hurt them, subconsciously we are teaching them they do not have a voice and there is something to be ashamed of. Especially in the Caribbean, parents love to say, "You are acting too grown. Shut your mouth. Out of order." There was no free speech as a child. I learned how to vacillate between two worlds; the one I desired and the one I despised. There was always a treasure hunt for the truth in my house. Everyone lied. Mummy fabricated her happiness, Smith masked his agony behind bottles of Appleton and Jay Wray and Nephews, and I pretended that home was perfect.

The older I got, the more ashamed I became about where I lived. The children at school were becoming more curious about my biological parents and Mummy's vagueness didn't help much.

"Child, why you so nosy?"

"I want to know what happened to her."

"She got sick."

"Sick how?"

"Jozanne, you ask too many questions!"

Since there were no answers to my mother's disappearance, I boasted about my father at recess.

"My father lives in America. He has a big house, a huge car and he buys me lots of things."

The little girls sat there listening in on this story with envy. We all longed to leave the dusty, pothole riddled roads and live in that magical city where dreams came true and miracles happened. America was our imagined land of "milk and honey." America was our Promised Land.

How was I going to conquer the world if home was so dysfunctional? My biological parents lived in two different countries and I had no relationship with either of them. They were only stories through the point of view of Mummy. An incomplete story. Disconnected. Broken. It was definitely not perfect.

But does the perfect home really exist? If it does, where is it? Who first introduced the concept of family and home? Where did this desire come from? We fought for it when we were kids and if we did not obtain it, our mission was to create it for ourselves. From birth this innate idea and expectation that home should be a certain way sticks with us. We all long for the place where we are welcomed, loved, and celebrated.

John Bradshaw, a family-systems therapy advocate and family dynamics expert, cites research that found 96 percent of all families are to some degree 'dysfunctional'—that is, the system by which the family interacts is distorted by the addictions and compulsions of one or more members, and so ignores the needs of each individual.

Can you relate? I can. To a time when home didn't feel safe anymore. My guardians had forgotten to stand guard at the doorway of their home and allowed an intruder to enter. For some, this intruder could have been drugs, alcohol, or infidelity. For me it was child abuse.

HOME

It was the beginning of me becoming jaded, cynical, and suspicious. Doubtful of good, fearful of love, and hardened by sin. My childlikeness and playfulness was locked away and guarded, vowing to never to be disappointed again. Trying my best to dissociate myself from the pain and defeat I experienced at home, for the rest of my young adult life I set out on a journey to be a better person than those who broke my heart. And with some form of success, I felt victorious. A conqueror. A winner. They were not going to get the best of me. But at twenty-three years old everything stopped. I was unable to go any further. I had no fight in me. I felt empty, afraid, and lonely.

It reminded me of a time in seventh grade when I decided to join the track team. I joined the team and I volunteered to be the runner for the 1500-meter race on sports day. I stood with all the other runners, ready for the race. My classmates and Mummy sat in the bleaches ready to cheer me on. The gun goes off. My classmates and teammates scream my name. "Go Jozanne! Go Jozanne!" I was running fast, passing all the other runners on the second lap. The only thing I forgot was not only had I not trained for this race, I had five more laps to go. On the third lap, with my heart beating out of my chest, legs hurting and feeling like I was going to faint, I stopped in the middle of the race and took a seat to catch my breath. I could not go any further. My classmates looking on with shock and rage. "Get up! What are you doing! Run!" But I just sat there. I couldn't run. I had run out of steam and the drive to win. I was not prepared for this kind of race. Just as I was not prepared for that race, I came to a point where it was obvious that my home life as a child did not prepare me to win as an adult.

There was a huge missing piece and it was called a "broken and abused childhood." Every abused woman at some point will run into that broken little girl. Let's call her "Sheila." Things will seem perfect for a moment and then "Sheila" shows up. Sheila is lost, afraid, angry, and wounded, dissatisfied with anyone who comes down her path. It is difficult for Sheila to receive love because she does not see herself as worthy. Sheila is stuck and has lost the drive to go any further in life.

Her broken childhood sometimes has her floating without any destination. When she takes one step forward, she finds herself going two steps backward. It's difficult to pinpoint her pain or even articulate it. It controls her thoughts, decisions, and relationships. Sheila has forgotten who she was created to be and the purpose of her existence. Her childhood trauma has gotten a hold of her. She wants to feel at home with herself and the people around her, but she can never find the peace she seeks.

These feelings are real and can ruin Sheila's life. I understand Sheila very well. I was once Sheila and sometimes Sheila tries to resurrect within me, but I have learned how to keep her in the grave where she belongs. The harder I deny Sheila the right to exist in my life, the less she shows up. Sheila is no longer invited to tag along on my journey, and with Sheila gone, I am able to see my true self, *and* live my best life.

For many years, I have searched to find "home" only to realize that the "home" I was in need of was not built with wood or bricks. Don't get me wrong, I am not advocating that having a wonderful family or a beautiful house should not be desired. It definitely has its place. However, I am campaigning *home* being more than a street address or the environment in which we were raised. If home was only where one lived, we wouldn't find people living in mansions and still feeling homeless. They hate turning the keys in the door after a long day's work and can't wait to get up and leave early the following day.

I have come across many individuals who by society's definition have "success" but are not happy. Depression, sadness, disappointment, and tragedy have taken their soul hostage.

Let's take a look at the story of Adam and Eve in the garden. The Garden of Eden was their home, a place of safety and abundance. They belonged there and were in need of nothing. They had identity, and were unashamed and unafraid. They knew God to be good. They had eternal security, access to God any time, and the confidence to approach Him. Instead of being fearful of his presence, they were confident in his love. A love relationship between God and man, relentless, passionate, and intimate. They were *home*. In this home, they ruled not out of possessiveness but out of purpose. Yet Scripture tells us one day the Serpent entered their home and caused them to lose not only their place of authority, but their place of identity.

Adam and Eve had lent their ears to the lies of the Serpent and in seconds they lost their home. What I find interesting about the text is that the "Garden" did not change. It was still perfect in beauty. Gorgeous vines, fragrant flowers, and everything good bloomed there. Yet they lost their *place* in the Garden. The Garden of Eden was still full of life and had everything in it to sustain them, yet they no longer were able to abide in its abundance because something on the inside had blinded their eyes from the truth. Their spiritual and emotional system became infected with a virus and their thought life did not make them capable of functioning from wholeness.

They still had the blue sky above them, were able to smell beautiful flowers, walk on carpet of living green, and enjoy the soothing sun. They literally had the freedom to occupy the Earth. They were not constrained or limited by width, height, or depth yet in their soul something made them see differently.

God was their father and made them rulers. He gave them dominion over everything. The order and harmony of creation spoke to them of God's infinite wisdom and power. But right there in the Garden, God was teaching one of His greatest lessons—that home has nothing to do with location but with disposition.

Just like our first parents, we are placed in this world. God has given to us many external blessings, yet still a lesson of all times is that true happiness is found not in the indulgence of luxury but in communion with God and others. If we no longer abide in God, the fruit of our lives becomes destitute and eventually we lose the ability to see who we are and why we are here clearly.

Those two had a relationship with God and knew who they were. They were Home. That was what God intended for every human being on this planet. An internal and unshakeable knowing about who we are leaves us limitless and able to thrive in an internal abundant life.

But despite the past, God showed us the way back to being whole. That was the main purpose for Jesus entering the world. *"Jesus is the way, the truth and the life."* Although God knew we would all encounter disappointments and pain, He had a plan set in advance to remind us that we are not unloved.

"For God so loved the world, He gave His one and only begotten son that whosoever believeth in Him should not perish but have everlasting life." John 3:16.

We've heard that scripture so many times, and most people equate that with Heaven and Hell. It is much deeper than that.

Everlasting life does not begin in our transition, it begins the minute we have the revelation of truth. It can begin now! We can be alive and yet be dead in our soul. Whether we live in Beverly Hills or the worst part of town, God is *greater* than our circumstances. For most of my life, home was a constant search due to my broken childhood. Since I was born I have moved twenty-one times in search of the perfect home, not knowing that the home I needed to focus on was the one between God and me. God wanted to take me back to the Garden of Eden, not literally but internally. It did matter where I was raised, nor who had done what to me, God was capable of transforming me from the inside out. He is ever competent in reminding us of His divine grace and giving us the capacity to love life with a continual increase.

Home is not luxury or even ambition. It is a spiritual disposition. Luke 17:20–21 says, *" The coming of the kingdom of God is not something that can be observed, nor will people say, 'Here it is,' or 'There it is,' because the kingdom of God is in you."* The more I found home inside of me, the greater it manifested in the physical, not just in material things but also in my emotional life. Everything we need in God, He has placed it on the inside of us.

We often go on a quest to find the invisible through visible things we can touch, feel, and see, only to discover it is never in multi-million-dollar houses, 401Ks, or fancy cars. Although those things are a blessing, still the material can never heal our internal wounds. Too often victims of broken homes remain handicapped, and if we are not careful, we can fall prey to the belief that we are incapable of success and a healthy emotional life because of our horrible home life as children. This is not the truth. For every believer, everything we need is in Christ Jesus. *"Therefore, if anyone who is in Christ, the new creation has come: The old has gone, the new is here!"* 2 Corinthians 5:17.

It is in Christ we are constantly gaining new treasures of knowledge, discovering fresh springs of happiness, and obtaining clearer conceptions of the immeasurable, unfailing love of God. In this Garden of Eden we are restored and lacking nothing. Home is a place where we are loved and invested in. It's a place of constant compassion, abounding grace, and relentless love.

Let's take a trip Home together.

CHAPTER 2

MOMMY DEAREST

MOTHER

A blank space was drawn next to your name
Words disappeared from my pen
A poet without a poem
I tried to paint a picture of our love
A bare canvas
Emotions caged by your absence
Expressions lost in this black hole
And it never beats for you.
MOTHER

Saddened by my cold–shoulder
Your name, an incomplete sentence on my lips
Left me too afraid to fight for you
I let you go for a moment
Because there was no You, it took forever to find me
And my way back to your arms
Seemed like eternity
MOTHER

MOMMY DEAREST

I prayed to God
Give me a glimpse of you
Light my path back to your cradled arms
Let me suck on your breast and it be sweet
Hold me like a gift
Love me like a baby's first kiss
And the missing part of me will arrive
I await you soon
MOTHER

You drifted off with the wind
I stood inside the ruined place of your existence
Mournful but awakened to the truth
Robbed of your innocence
Jailed in your silence
Death stole all the moments
For you are free and my purpose is evident
I grabbed life by the throat and breathe into the ashes of
your grave
Live again
I speak for you mother.
MOTHER

ON SEPTEMBER 22, 2016, I received the phone call every child dreads. It was an ordinary day driving home from work when the area code 876 popped up on my caller ID. A call from Jamaica meant two things; either my mother needed money or she had passed away. That day I knew my mother had died. A few months prior to this call I had a dream. In it, she was the most radiant I'd ever seen her. Love exuded from her eyes and her arms were open wide to receive me. "I am sorry for any way I've hurt you, Jozanne," she said.

Speechless, I collapsed in her arms, weeping. As I wept, I realized I had needed her love all my life. When I woke up from the dream, I was crying profusely. Her time among us was short and I had an inner knowing. It had been fifteen years since I had seen her face to face. For all those years our relationship was bound only through phone conversations and letters. Our routine was, I would call the hospital, the receptionist would answer, and they would call for Jean to come to the phone. I could hear her voice in the distance as she made way to the phone. Not knowing her temperament, I braced myself for whatever mood she might be in that day. The conversation normally began like this:

"Hi, Jean."

"Hey, Jossy."

"How are you?"

"Fine."

"How are you feeling?"

"Fine."

An awkward pause normally came at this moment. We did not know where to go from there. Our mother-daughter relationship was stuck at where we left it over thirty years ago. Too much time had passed. Our lives were so different, as if we were strangers. The only thing that broke the discomfort was the list of items she named for me to send her. I would write them down on whatever piece of paper I found that moment.

"Jossy, can you buy me some brassieres?"

"Sure."

"I need a bag for church."

"Okay."

"New shoes as well."

"Okay, I will send it in the mail."

It was our routine. We each needed to feel some form of normalcy. Although sometimes I could not afford her requests, I still wrote them down. Every now and then the monotony of our conversation changed. Jean would give a quick burst of laughter and share some random story. Like the day one of the mentally ill patients stole her Bible and escaped through the window with it. We laughed so hard that day. Those times were like a sunny day during winter. It was a gift from Heaven to remind me that deep down in my mother's soul lived a woman the world didn't know. Other than those moments, however, we lived in the silence. The silence between us was loaded with secrecy and shame. Most times I found myself censoring the conversation to prevent old wounds from being provoked. While we both needed to let go of the past, distance and shame magnified it more.

The morning after the dream I lay on my bed numb, wishing I loved her more. I had reached the place of peace and maturity where I wanted to see her again. Seven months later she was gone. Writer Susan Wiggs says, *"There is something about losing a mother that is permanent and inexpressible—a wound that will never quite heal."* That left me thinking how much pain I have lived in, because even though my mom was alive, I never had her in my life. Now she was gone from this Earth.

The month of May will come and the color pink will line the card aisle at the supermarket. It's Mother's Day again and we get to celebrate our mothers' sacrifices and love. We remember the way they held our hands when we took our first step, taught us how to say "Mama," and kissed our boo boos when we hurt ourselves. Once again I face the deep sadness of an absent mother and sometimes the indifference of friends and relatives that never asked about her. Not speaking about her did not make her invisible; it made her the elephant in the room that everyone ignored.

From a child's birth, its first cry into the world beckons for the safety of a mother's embrace. This little one's desire is to be reassured that in this new world they will be taken care of. A mother's cradling arms calms her baby's fear and the sound of her voice quiets its anxious spirit. The cushion of her breast brings comfort and as the child grows, a mother's wisdom and love nurtures them to have a sense of belonging and a feeling of safety.

To her child, she is unforgettable and no one can replace her. Yet today in many homes across the world, children are motherless due to different circumstances. The absence of a mother leaves a child confused and at blame that somehow they played a part in Mommy's disappearance. Research on BrandonGaille.com concludes that *"Children that come from motherless homes have difficulties developing bonds with other adults and there is an increased level of fear and anxiety that is present with children from motherless homes because they are scared that other adults will also leave."*

Although I rarely spoke about my mother growing up, in the quiet of the night I often wondered about her absence. Regardless of the fact that I knew she was sick in the hospital, knowing her on a first name basis did not make it easier to digest. Eventually my resentment grew into numbness, and by the time I was six years old, I no longer wanted to see her. Mummy thought differently.

Mummy became adamant about me visiting Jean at the hospital. Sunday after Sunday, she badgered me, "Jozanne, you need to visit your mother."

"Why did she leave in the first place" was my response.

"She is sick," Mummy replied.

I was determined not to go, but Mummy was not going to take no for an answer. After church one Sunday, Mummy sat me down on the bed. "You are going to see your mother today," she said firmly. Jean's dinner was already packed in a plastic container and a jar filled with freshly made carrot juice was placed in the bag along with it. That Sunday I followed Mummy, complaining and grumbling all the way to the hospital.

On the trip I tried conjuring up some form of sentiment to feel "normal" and remove the guilt of my cold heart towards Jean. The five mile walk in the sun from our house to the hospital felt like eternity.

Two security guards stood watch at the hospital gate. The sign above our heads read "Bellevue Hospital." This was the place where crazy people were sent; the kids at school had told me. I could not believe this was where my mother lived.

Barbed wired fences surrounding the compound made it look like a prison. A few patients wandered in the yard and when they saw strangers, they stopped and stared. Mummy held my hand tightly. "Stop staring at them, they hate that," she scolded. Some of the small gravel from the yard jumped into my sandals and made it uncomfortable for me to walk. We were headed towards C-Ward, where the most volatile patients were locked away. The closer I got to the facility, the more afraid I became.

A nurse in a well-ironed pink and white uniform came out to greet us.

"Howdy, Ms. Dixon, so glad to see you here every Sunday."

"Hi, Nurse Campbell, how is Jeanie doing?"

"Not so well this week. We had to put her on extra medication."

Turning her attention to me, the nurse was astonished at how much I had grown. It seemed as if everyone knew about me even though I never met them before. "Jean is going to be so glad to see her!"

We followed Nurse Campbell into the building and one of the nurses in a matching uniform, called down the hallway, "Jean! Jean, your mother is here to see you!" Walking down the hallway, the patients behind bars laughed aloud, while others screamed at the top of their voices and made strange sounds. One of the patients yelled out, "Miss Dixon, did you bring anything for me today?"

"Next time, Audrey," Mummy said.

Audrey stretched her hands through the bars, reaching for me. "Is that Jean's daughter? Hey pretty little girl. I like your hat."

"Stop being nosy," Nurse Campbell admonished.

BEAUTIFUL

I clutched Mummy's frock even tighter as we hurried down the hallway.

When we got to Jean's cell, my nineteen-year-old mother sat curled up on her bed in the corner, gawking at us, her skin flawless and her long, curly hair disheveled as if she'd just rolled out of bed. Nurse Campbell took me by the hand and placed me in front of her cell. "Jeanie, your daughter is here to see you" Jean did not respond. "Jozanne, tell your mother how old you are."

"Six," I said apprehensively.

Once again Jean said nothing. She sat there staring at me, her eyes cold and distant. It felt like she was a lion confined behind bars and I was her prey. Any moment she would pounce on me and rip me a part. Trying to appease Jean, Mummy nervously pulled the stuff she bought from the bag.

"Jeanie, I bought you some nice smelling soap, toilet paper, and sweet pomade for your hair." Breaking a half smile, Jean asked, "Did you bring me any food?"

"Yes, Jeanie, your favorite, stew peas and rice."

Mummy handed her all the goodies between the steel bars. I waited for her acknowledgement but she stayed busy searching through the bags. We watched her suck the juice from the pig's tail and lick her fingers. Then she spoke.

"Are you being a good girl, Jossy?" Stunned by her acknowledgement all I could do was nod. Yes, I was being a good girl.

Decked out in a perfectly fitting yellow dress my dad sent from the States, I stood there speechless and ashamed that this was where my mother lived. Looking into her dark eyes my knees trembled, and her silence cut through my being like a knife. The feeling of neglect and abandonment crept into my heart and once again shame reared its ugly head. Right there I came up with the perfect lie I was going to tell my classmates if asked about her whereabouts. "My mother lives in Florida and she works as a flight attendant." This was going to be my story and I stuck to it for the next ten years.

Jean continued wolfing down the rest of her food. Afterwards she became dauntingly quiet and everything Mummy said she replied repetitively, "Yeah…yeah…yeah." It was as if she was stuck at ten years old. Her chilling gaze from under her eyebrows made me aware she was angry with me, but I had no clue the reason she seemed so volatile.

Mummy initiated more conversation but Jean's attention remained fastened on me. Like a raging bull she charged from her bed and rushed to the steel bars, pointing her finger straight at me. "GET HER AWAY FROM ME. I DON'T WANT TO SEE HER." She banged her body against the bars. "Mummy, I want to come home," Jean begged. Standing there completely bewildered and terrified, I held Mummy's skirt tighter.

The nurses rushed down the hallway and into Jean's cell. One nurse injected her with a needle and her legs gave way beneath her like spaghetti. I stood there frozen as if I had come in contact with a monster. Mummy grabbed my hand. "Let's go, Jozanne!" We rushed down the hallway.

"Little girl!" Audrey yelled from her cell. "I like your hat!"

As we rushed through the hallways, Jean's screams got louder. "MUMMY! MUMMY! I WANT TO GO HOME! TAKE ME HOME!"

The walk back home engulfed in a thick silence spoke volumes. There were secrets hidden and I was too young and afraid to inquire why my mother lived in a mental institution and why she hated me. There was clearly more to the story than everyone was telling me. Mummy's response to all my questions was to pray and God would take care of it.

My grandmother had faith that God was still in the healing business and anytime now He was going to grant Jean a miracle. One day Jean was going to come home and everything was going to be back to normal. "There is nothing impossible for God to do," was Mummy's mantra. From that day on at 5am every morning, Mummy climbed over Smith and knelt at the bedside praying relentlessly for Jean's healing.

Shortly after that visit, my desire to live with my father intensified. Periodically, I questioned Mummy why Jean was in the hospital. She would smile and say, "Child, God and time will answer all your questions. Just keep living." Still, it was imperative that I got those answers because the kids at school were getting more curious about my mother's whereabouts. Yet there were no answers to the brokenness and confusion creeping into my soul, so I kept silent and masked my grief.

Although my mother was absent from my life, I deeply missed her. Despite the façade I displayed, I wanted my mother home. For example, a person who is born without arms and legs doesn't necessarily miss their limbs because they never had them in the first place, but it doesn't mean they don't experience the difficulty of not having them. Having their hands and legs would make life much easier. Those who are born without limbs have no other choice but to discover their own way to exist and thrive in his world.

Although I was fortunate to have arms and legs, I still had my own handicap. I needed to figure out who I was in this world without the care of my mother. Everything about womanhood was wrapped up in her. She was meant to be a gift to my growth in this life. Her words were meant to soothe the lies the world would tell me about beauty. Her arms meant for comfort when my heart was broken by boys who only saw me as an object. Yet how was I going to be a woman in this life without her presence when she despised everything about me?

Mummy had a different memory of Jean.

JEAN

She was a delicate lily,
Soft, sweet, silent
One of a kind.
When she smiled roses bloomed

The sun moved.
Tender
Eloquent
Mysterious and Elegant
The pride of a mother's heart
Handled with a velvet glove
Spotless.
Jean Maureen Ashley
Soft, sweet, silent

This gentle woman was not the woman I met. The Jean I knew was violent and angry. It was obvious she had a bone to pick with me. Being in a home where sensitive issues were rarely discussed created emotional distance and many false identities.

In the *Daily Signal* it is stated that, *"Eighty-six percent of African American children unfortunately do not live with both parents."* There are many reasons why one or both parents may be absent, such as divorce, avoidance of responsibilities, or unfortunately, death. Whatever the reason, the child suffers. The disappearance of a parent most times leaves a child with abandonment issues.

Shame is always what we feel when the moral law of love is broken. The love of a parent plays a vital role in a child's life and how they will show up in the world. The reason why a parent is incapable of taking care of the child is irrelevant. Whether it is a drug addicted mother or a deadbeat father, a child will always question God why. Why are my parents on welfare? Why am I the black sheep of the family? Why am I treated unfairly among my siblings? Why was I born into poverty? Sometimes there are no answers.

I spent many years asking why until I learned to instead ask "How?" How do I show up in the world without my mother? What kind of woman am I going to be? Who will I glean from to grow? I needed to make a decision in my life. Was I going to use the excuse of my mother's absence and become a powerless and broken woman? Scripture told me, *"Before I formed you in the womb I knew you, before you were born I set you apart."* Jeremiah 1:5. Notwithstanding the household in which we were raised, we all are set apart for a deeper and more significant purpose. So your mother was a drug addict. She prostituted herself, got pregnant, and you came into the world. She left you on your grandmother's doorstep and went on with her life. It's not my intention to be insensitive, but if we continue to stay stuck in the whys, the hows remain impossible. Every calamitous event of our lives is no surprise to the Almighty God. There is a higher purpose that extends far beyond our DNA. It is capable of standing on its own, thriving beyond the storms and living despite the death it faces.

Across the world, within the privacy of their homes every family struggles with some form of dysfunction. Some are more severe than others. Yet no matter how much we attempt to lean on our own understanding, we don't always get the right answers to comfort the disappointments we experience.

The question becomes, do we allow a horrible childhood to dictate our future? What if I told you that the ultimate fate of every human being in this world is not attached only to the family they were raised in, that our final destination of true identity ultimately goes back to the Creator of all things—God? *"God is the author and finisher of our faith."* Hebrews 12:2.

Hear me out for a moment. Family is a great institution God set in place to teach children about love. *"Jesus grew in wisdom and stature, and in favor with God and men."* Luke 2:52. within the nurturing care of his Earthly parents. Parenthood reveals God's character. It is where we learn responsibility, respect for authority, forgiveness, and the building of character and love.

As you know, we don't always have the luxury of living in homes with guardians that bear those qualities. The outcome of living in an abusive, uncaring, and neglectful home has a strong effect on children, that can lead them to a place of rebellion, hostility, and unbelief in a loving God.

The lack of my mother's presence came with some unhealthy decisions in my life. Decisions like being in toxic friendships, accepting abuse, and turning to anyone who showed me love, even if they were not good for me.

One thing I can say is a mother's embrace is worth more than a thousand hugs from strangers. In her bosom lies the unconditional love of our Heavenly Father. There is nothing sweeter than her loving arms, yet sometimes life denies us the wealth of her cradle. The loss of a mother is difficult to endure. It is a pain that lingers with us for a long time. God is able to heal and comfort our broken hearts.

Throughout scripture God does not portray Himself as only male but expresses, *"Humankind was created as God's reflection: in the divine image God created them; female and male, God made them."* While often we perceive God's Spirit as masculine only, that is not fully the truth. In scripture, God is portrayed *"Like the eagle that stirs up its nest, and hovers over its young, and God spreads wings to catch us."* Deuteronomy 32:11–12. We tend to concentrate more on God's masculine traits and rarely think about God as a comforting mother. In Isaiah 66:13, God reminds us, *"As a mother comforts her child, so I will comfort you."*

Beloved, we shall be comforted wherever we are because God's Spirit cares for the fatherless, and the motherless. He discerns our thoughts and knows the areas in our lives that need nurturing. God is compared to a nursing mother: *"Can a woman forget her nursing child, or show no compassion for the child of her womb? Even these may forget, yet I will not forget you."* Isaiah 49:15. It brings me much comfort to know God never forgets us. He remembers the orphans, the abandoned, and the rejected.

When a parent abandons a child, children equate that experience with being forgotten by God. Loneliness sets in, and that child wanders throughout the world aimlessly, feeling no sense of stability or assurance that they are loved. It becomes difficult to trust others, and they avoid deep, meaningful relationships to guard their heart from being hurt again.

Our creator has a plan for our lives despite the disappearance of a biological mother. God is fully capable of giving us spiritual mothers that will mentor and pour into our lives what we lack from our biological mother. I have been extremely fortunate to be mentored by fantastic women who inspire me and who have been catalysts to help shape me into the woman I am today.

Remember in the first chapter I mentioned choice? At some point we all have to make a choice about who we will become. I realized at some point in my life I had to make a decision to either focus on who was missing or on who was present.

"Relatives" does not always mean "family." Sometimes God grants us a family of our own that loves us as if their blood ran through our veins. Over the years God has send me wonderful sisters, like my good friends, Dalia Phillips, Andrea Navedo, Belle Bromfield, LaTonya Lewis and many more that not only inspire me but walked by side through many tough seasons where I thought I could not make it.

My spiritual mother and friend in the faith, Joy Bohlinger, is a Godsend. She exemplifies, grace, love, and sacrifice. From her I have been able to glean wisdom, walk in truth and become a fearless woman. Take hold of these relationships and realize that we may not always be able to change the past, but we can always embrace the gifts God gives us now. *Now* is the most powerful moment in our lives. It is the deciding factor where faith comes alive and obedience manifests into a miracle. Yesterday does not exist, only *now*. Although the past often leaves its tentacles in our hearts, if we can grab the moment of *now*, the past becomes just that, our past.

God is capable of working all things together for our good. *"For the Lord is close to the brokenhearted and saves those who are crushed in spirit."* Psalms 34:11. The same thing that the enemy used to persecute us God uses to preserve us. The greatest miracle God has ever done and is still performing today is turning our brokenness into His splendor.

Our coming into this world is not an accident. Purpose is attached to each breath, but this comes with us surrendering our ways, our ideas of how life should look, and partnering with God on purpose. *Your* purpose. Not your mother's or father's, but *your* purpose.

From the second we are born, we crave connection with that which we came out of. Umbilical cords get cut, but souls stay tied. I never knew my fears ran so deep until I watched many people swimming upstream to love me and I always managed to find a way to go under water. Because of my mother's absence, there was no use getting saved only to be thrown overboard again. For many years my heart rejected the love from those God placed in my path because I was unwilling to let go of past hurts and who I wanted my parents to be.

Whenever we spend time focusing on our past hurts, we end up rejecting God's current blessings and sabotaging our joy. As a person of faith, the only way I discovered the true me was to run into the arms of the One who heals, Jesus. His name is Yahweh, which means, "I Am" in Hebrew. I love that name," I AM." In Him lies the names of all our needs. *I AM* whatever you need. *I AM* your strength, your comfort, your peace, and your certainty. You can bet on Me every time. *I AM* whatever you need me to be in your life. He is the creator whose character is flawless. He is approachable and trustworthy. He is absolute in truth, goodness, and beauty.

I AM will always lead us beside still waters and restore our souls from the pangs of abandonment. The events that took place in your life can have you running away from all that is good. It does not have to be that way. Today we can recover joy because every promise in God is "Yes and Amen." Isaiah 61:3 says, *"He will provide for those who grieve in Zion, bestow on them a crown of beauty instead of ashes, the oil of gladness instead of mourning, a garment of praise instead of despair. You shall be called oaks of righteousness, a planting of the Lord for the display of his splendor."* While we might not be able to undo the past, God has a way of restoring our lives where we are able to move on and flourish.

No one born into this world asked to be here. We all enter, and when we do, we don't know the circumstances in which we will find ourselves. Some of us are born with a silver spoon in our mouths and others have to fight our way to even have a seat at the table. Those without spoons, like me, had to learn how to let go of entitlement and enjoy my unique path. The worst thing we can do with our lives is compare it to others'. We are all given something to overcome, some greater than others. The only way to have victory is to know we are dealt this hand because God has equipped us to handle it.

In some weird way the absence of my mother in my life gave me the gift of gratefulness. It taught me to value the people in my life. Nothing and no one should be taken for granted. It taught me to savor every moment, knowing that life is not an accident but designed to manifest God's glory.

On October 21, 2016, I travelled to Jamaica and buried my mother in a colorful Catholic church in the heart of Kingston, Jamaica. The nuns entered the church carrying her coffin. Sitting in the front row, I was unwilling to look at her face in the coffin. I needed to remember her the way I saw her in the dream. There were no family members present. God had brought me to this ruined place to give her the greatest honor. I sang along softly with the choir as everyone gave glory for her life. I tried to make sense of it all. Was this her purpose? To have one child, live in a mental institution all her life, and then die? Where was the glory in that? There I stood among the poor, the broken, and the rejected patients. They too were left alone.

Once again God used me to hug strangers, never allowing me to hug the mother who carried me in her womb. In my carnal mind, I saw many reasons to be angry, and rightfully so, but beyond the death and disappointment I saw the beauty. Jean's life was more than being confined to a mental hospital. She had a purpose, and I was a big part of it. Not something you want to think when your heart is broken.

Yet I couldn't help feeling her presence when I hugged each patient in the hospital.

Earlier that day I had sat on her bed, neatly made as if she knew she would not return. The patients consoled me with the stories she shared about all the times we spoke. Jean had left a legacy and I needed to accept that I was a treasure, even when I could not see it. I felt like I had not done enough. It saddened me that I was incapable of fixing the situation. Then God reminded me that I was one of her greatest accomplishment. I was the jewel God made from her brokenness and it humbled me. Tears flooding my face, I stared at the statue of Mother Mary on the wall in front of me.

"Unless a grain of wheat falls to the ground and dies, it stands alone. But if it dies, it produces much grain." John 12:24. My mother was out of the body but her legacy lived in me. She had purpose and had made her mark in the world behind those bars at Bellevue Hospital. Her life had value. She was significant to all the women who received healing through the telling of her story. She was remembered in the hearts of all the women I performed in my solo play, *Beautiful*. Somehow it all made sense. I was her offspring and God had a plan. A new day was on the horizon.

The outlook of our lives changes when we see through the lenses of Heaven. In my humanity, I felt abandoned and rejected. But in my divinity, I was set apart for a greater purpose, not only to bring God glory but to bring my mother honor.

After the service we made our way down to May Pen Cemetery. We sang several hymns and as I took a shovel and threw the dirt on her coffin, her death reminded me that it is not how we come into the world that makes a difference but how we depart from it that truly matters. I was my mother's daughter, and although we only had maybe one hug in my lifetime, she had left her signature through my birth.

This seems too lofty to even mention but I am proud to be my mother's daughter. The shame I once felt at age six no longer lives. From the eyes of Heaven, Jean Ashley lived. All the stories I heard of her did not depict the woman who had me running down the hallway terrified. She brought joy to all the other patients. She served, she prayed, she shared her own testimony within the walls of the hospital. Now I get to share her testimony to the world. Jean Maureen Ashley died on September 22, 2016 but made so many women alive.

A mother is a precious gift from God, and while sometimes we don't get the opportunity to enjoy that gift due to circumstance, it does not mean they didn't serve their purpose in our lives. Maybe not the way we desire or hope they should, but trust me, when we look with the eyes of Heaven, they served us well and God gets the glory.

Perspective changes everything.

CHAPTER 3

DON'T SETTLE

IN THE BOOK of Exodus chapter 32, we hear the story of the children of Israel after they leave Egypt on their way to the Promised Land. It wasn't a long time after God delivered them from a cruel leader who held them in bondage, yet they found themselves at a place where doubt and fear obstructed their spiritual sight to the promise and they settled for a golden calf.

The Israelites had seen the salvation of the Lord as they came upon the impassable barrier set before them. God had given them divine direction, and though fearful as they must have been, God did not fail to provide a way out of the pickle in which they found themselves when their past came rushing in with a vengeance to overtake them. God was ready to demonstrate His power that He was worthy of their trust. God's deliverance was an expression of His heart. He did not want His children to settle anymore under the bondage of their past, but believe in Him for the best. The Promised Land was His best and He would do anything necessary to get them there.

Once delivered by a Mighty God and led miraculously through what seems impossible for them to accomplish, the children of Israel found themselves worshipping a golden calf. Although the Israelites were destined for greatness, they were willing to settle for less than what God had planned for their lives. They became tired of waiting and soon doubt set in that God would keep His word.

At one point or another we all tend to settle. Just like the Israelites we become impatient. We lose faith that there is better ahead than the

Egypt we escaped from and soon we find ourselves in the cycle of old patterns once again. The faith we once had slowly begins to dwindle. Life seems hopeless again and we become discouraged. Soon, we find ourselves in places we shouldn't be.

Those of us who come from an abusive background so often end up going on a journey to find love and acceptance in lifeless things. The only difference is our idols are not made of gold, they are made of flesh with no spirit. They promise us freedom; we look to them for love, peace, and affirmation. These are the Mr. and Mrs. Wrong in our lives. We believe they will heal our childhood wounds and we settle in worship.

I have found myself in this toxic cycle on countless occasions. The sad legacy of child abuse often results in abusive relationships. It becomes our drug of choice. In a weird way, the high of drama and chaos makes us feel alive, though soon we come down of its ecstasy and plunge into the pit of heartbreak all over again. This chapter is dedicated to those who find themselves always falling for the wrong men.

Choosing the right mate can be difficult, especially when there are no examples to compare it to. As a teenager, I was hasty when it came to dating. If he was cute, had a nice smile, and gave me attention, he could claim me as his. Without the knowledge of how valuable we are to God, we will settle for anything.

When we don't give ourselves time to heal, we find ourselves settling for contracts rather than the covenant promise. Old, unhealed wounds lead us into the arms of idols that have no life. Child abuse victims are oftentimes prone to abusive relationships. Without a conscious mindset to change, we fall prey to people who are not emotionally available or just as abusive as our past perpetrator. Settling always stems from old patterns.

I was raised in a house where I saw my grandmother settle for an abusive relationship. This example in my life defined how I would interact with men and what I accepted from them. My familiarity with brokenness made it normal for me to settle for less.

When we forfeit our healing process to wholeness, the final result will end up in sadness. I witnessed the melancholy look on Mummy's face when I was a child. Although Smith became her lifejacket, life-jackets with holes can never take us ashore; they will deflate and eventually both will go under.

Mummy always spoke about leaving Smith, who came home from work most evenings drunk, cussing and carrying on like he did the night before.

WOMAN DO THIS, WOMAN DO THAT

Woman do this
Woman do that

I don't like what you cook
I don't like that hat

Woman come here
Woman go there

I don't like that dress
And please, fix your hair

Woman I love you
Woman I hate you.

I don't like who you are
I don't like what you do

Woman do this
Woman do that.

BEAUTIFUL

The nosy neighbors had a field day eavesdropping and peeking through their windows after each fight between Smith and Mummy. The fear of our dysfunction being exposed was like a haunting shadow over our heads. The harder we tried to cover the shame, the more it was exposed. Growing up in an environment where my guardians pretended all was well taught me not to tell the truth. Everyone needed to believe we were doing just fine. Fear was the culprit in our home.

It is said that "perfect love cast out all fear." Yet most of the world operates from a place of fear. We are afraid of people different from us, so we oppress them. We are afraid of the unknown, so we don't move from complacency. We are afraid of things we don't understand, so we discount its credibility. We are afraid of too much truth, so we cling to political correctness. The majority of the pain the world suffers stems from a place of fear. If we take a closer look, we will discover our problems most of the time stem from fear.

Mummy was afraid to leave Smith because she was not sure how to make it on her own. He was the breadwinner. He took care of the bills and provided us with shelter. It did not matter that his language was abusive, since he had some charming qualities that made her stay and had me believing he would treat Mummy better one day.

Smith was the only father figure I knew. Every Friday evening after work Smith brought me home two hot Jamaican beef patties, and after dinner we took a stroll down the street to the neighborhood bar.

"Hey, Leroy, give this girl a kola champagne!" he yelled across the counter as he propped me up on the barstool.

I usually took his left over change and went to the jukebox to play my favorite song, "One Love" by the legendary Bob Marley. The bar was misty from cigarette smoke, blurring out the drunken old men attempting to dirty dance with loose girls who conned them out of their money after their third drink. As the music played, I imitated the girls' dirty whine. It made Leroy laugh every time. "Go, rude girl," he would cheer as he poured Smith his fifth glass of rum and Pepsi.

The walk home was always eventful, to say the least. Smith staggered from one side of the street to the next, singing, Yellow Man's, *Getting Married* at the top of his voice. Women would yell through their windows, "Shut up you drunk!" That was his favorite song, yet he showed no interest in marrying Mummy, which she desperately wanted for many reasons, especially to impress her sister, Pastor Carmen Taylor.

Pastor Carmen Taylor was Mummy's oldest sister of three children from Trelawney. She was an evangelist regal, chic and soft-spoken. It took three buses to get to her enormous house in the posh Red Hills neighborhood where the grass and trees had a haircut by some white guy. Unlike our two rooms, her four bedroom house was a mansion. Everything she had, she owned. Her two pit bulls and a German shepherd viciously rushed to the gate, barking. We waited patiently for Pastor Carmen to make an entrance in her expensive housedress, every hair neatly in place.

She would command the dogs away, locking them in the backyard. "Good to see you both," she said, refined and dignified.

I jumped into her arms. "Hi, Auntie!"

"Jozanne, you always wear the most beautiful dresses."

Mummy made sure if it. She wanted Pastor Carmen to know we too could be just as prim and proper. Pastor Carmen hugged me tightly and whispered in my ear, "God loves you, Jozanne."

To me *she* was like a God. I wanted to be just like her. She was well-travelled, respected, and owned her own home with the best of everything. Unlike us she had no lack. I could not wait to run my fingers along the keys of her beautiful Oakwood piano in the living room.

As a traveling evangelist she brought back "American treats" like Rice Krispies and Wrigley's gum. Whenever she knew we were coming, the dining table was neatly set with a peanut butter and jelly sandwich, a glass of milk, and a peach fruit cup just for me. While she and Mummy sat in the living room whispering conversation, I'd sneak back into the kitchen, open the refrigerator, and look at the abundance of food.

"God gets all the glory for everything," she always said.

I often wondered why God's glory was always in her house and not ours. Mummy too was a friend of Jesus just like her. Mummy worshipped the ground her sister walked. She was one of the reasons Mummy stayed with Smith. Pastor Carmen continuously reminded her, "Lorris, you know the Lord hates fornication. You need to get married to this man."

"He is a drunk, Carmen," Mummy would say.

"Well leave him then."

"Where am I going to go?"

"Well, God hates sin, so marry him."

I guess she thought if Smith put a ring on it that meant he would treat Mummy better. But no diamond ring can turn a man's heart into gold. Ladies, not everyone who likes it is mature enough to put a ring on it. He must like it, but additionally, he must respect, honor, and protect it. Although Smith cared about Mummy he was not going to go the full distance of love to win her heart. When we settle for less, the people we settle for will only give us what we think we are worth.

Many women compromise their standards, desires, and convictions in exchange for companionship. A friend of mine, Susanna Santiaga, once told me, "Know your needs versus your wants. You can live without your wants, but never without your needs." It is wise to take time and assess the relationship we desire to be in for the rest of our lives. Too many times women rush into a marriage for the wrong reasons. Some think marriage will make them happy, provide financial stability, and validate them. Ladies, just because a man comes along and says "I love you" and takes you on a few dates to a fancy restaurant doesn't mean he is marriage material.

God has given us the power to choose and the freedom to say *no*. It's alright to say, "Sir, I thank you for your time. I am sure you are an amazing person, but not quite the right one for me." Keep it moving.

If he is acting crazy most of the time but still brings you flowers, I say *run*! Flowers can't heal wounds. In the Christian community there are many broken and battered wives who live under the umbrella of "First Ladies" but are last on their husband's priority list when it comes to respect and love. I am not ignoring the fact that marriage takes work and sometimes deep love is birthed from weathered storms, hence the Cross.

However, I must address that women are not made to be doormats or punching bags in "the name of the Lord." I grew up watching my grandmother's emotions controlled. It did not matter how joyful she was, if Smith was not in a great mood, there went the rest of the day. When you find yourself in a relationship, especially before marriage, where someone sucks the joy out of you daily, pick up your joy and carry yourself home. Mummy knew leaving Smith was the best thing to do, but religion can keep us in bondage. Too often in the Christian community we hear, "Women are subjected to the 'man.'" We wait to be picked, but we are not products, like going to a shoe store and saying, "I like that orange one. Give me that." Ladies, we have the right to turn down offers no matter how old we are. Just like a shoe, just because he likes it, doesn't mean it will fit.

My grandmother held on to a toxic relationship in the hopes that things would get better. She nagged and frowned over Smith's excuses when it came to marriage.

"We don't have much money," he would say.

"Let's do it in a few years."

"It's not that important, it's just a piece of paper."

"We love each other, that's all that matters."

How many times have we heard those lame excuses? Regardless, my grandmother waited and waited until she settled for a situation that turned her into a different person, and a depressed woman. I must be honest, ladies; most of our heartbreaks are a result of our egos. "I can fix him." Sometimes we prefer to live in pain rather than accept that we were wrong. God has never called anyone to be our *everything.*

BEAUTIFUL

Relationships are great but they take work, and the ugly truth is, sometimes they do not work out. Most times women stay in abusive relationships because we don't want to feel like we have failed at our "womanly duties." Others stay in contumelious relationships out of convenience, and most stay because they have become comfortable with abuse. It is never God's intention for any human being to be enslaved by another.

When a man finds a good wife, he not only gets companionship, he gets favor with God, for in her are treasures no one else can grant him in his journey. *"She lacks nothing of value. She brings him good and not harm, all the days of her life."* Proverbs 31:12.

As you can see, however, there is a condition applied. I did not say his girlfriend, side-chick, or baby mama. I said his *wife*. Because we are not schooled on our worth at a young age, we often give away our merchandise for free. And this does not just pertain to sex only, but to our time, energy and resources. The problem is we don't believe we have value. Ladies, the next time you go to a Dollar Tree, please show me the aisle where diamonds are on the shelves. You will not find them there. Diamonds have to be sought out. Diamonds are not at everyone's disposal. They are placed in a glass case and you can look but not touch. Exquisite jewelry is not easily accessible. You have to go to a special store to find them, no one can walk into Tiffany's or Harry Winston's and pick up a diamond ring and try it on. You have to ask permission from the store owner.

Furthermore, mostly rich people will even enter the store. Either they have saved up or are just darn wealthy and decided they wanted to purchase this impeccable piece of jewelry. They come prepared and pretty much know exactly what they want before they enter. This leads me to my next point. Ladies, make sure the man you entertain is equipped with truth and love hidden in his heart and qualifies for what treasures are placed inside of you. Not every person who comes into our lives and admires us knows our value.

If we present ourselves cheaply to others, we can't expect to be respected in the relationship. We must evaluate whether or not this person spent quality time in the presence of God. Are they prepared to be a spouse? Ask him about his vision. You cannot help-meet one who does not have a vision. Where is he going? Do you plan on going there with him? If he has no vision all he is going to do is drag you through his confusion and unplanned future.

Just as the storeowner values his merchandise, God has extreme value in us. The storeowner of expensive jewels does not give easy access to customers because he knows how much he invested in the product. He has a standard value and anyone who enters the store must be prepared to live up to the requirements. God feels the same way about His children. He has a standard and He is not willing to be bargained with, nor is he willing to mark down His value. We must not be so accessible.

If you have toiled in your education, sought healing, and learned how to be financially stable, why would you ask someone who has no vision to be in your life? Notice I did not say a person who has no money. Money doesn't make a person, purpose does. If someone has vision and is willing to fulfill their purpose, they are going places. If we know who we are and see value in ourselves, we will take the time needed to consider all relationships.

My grandmother stayed and endured the physical fights, Smith's constant verbal abuse, and the cold silence that manipulated her emotions. Although she frequently threatened to leave, she never did. Witnessing this behavior at a young age came with consequences. It taught me that whatever abuse a man dished out to a woman, she deserved it. It was her job to make sure his temper was cool and his fist unclenched. Her voice had no significance and she was not worthy of true love.

We were nothing like the Huxtables for sure, and comparing myself to other kids in school did not help. The majority of my peers lived with both parents, and if there was any squabble in their house, no one knew about it. These inner affirmations were one day going to lead me to a place of co-dependency, anger, and resentment.

Many evenings I sat on the front steps, patiently waiting for Mummy to disclose the hidden things she whispered to Pastor Taylor. She only kept repeating the same old stories about her lost love, Colin. I was eager to know why my mother hated me and why my father was living three thousand miles away, but once again silence and secrets were the result.

Parents think their children's only concern is to eat, sleep, and play. However, children are much more in tune with their emotions than we think. Although it is difficult to articulate, a child does feel the unspoken words by the adults around them. They are very in tune to their environment. The only difference is, children are taught to not question or voice these feelings.

"You are too young to understand."

"You are acting older than your age."

"Leave mature people's business alone."

Parents will say, "I am protecting my child," but children have questions and I believe if we train our children to be honest with their feelings when they are young, we will see fewer gang members, runaway teenagers, and victims of cyclical abuse.

It's important to speak with our children about relevant issues, and lend a listening ear to what worries them. Open communication within a family produces trust among each other, and in the long run it gives our children the confidence to be who they are. This foundation will help them to know they have worth, and as a result, they will not settle for anything but God's best once on their own. *"Train up a child in the way he should go: and when he is old, he will not depart from it."* Proverbs 22:6.

To "train" means to "teach (a person or animal) a particular skill or type of behavior through practice and instruction over a period of time." If we fail to set the example of a healthy relationship in our homes, we are teaching our children this is their only possibility. Whenever we settle and compromise our worth, more than likely our children will perpetuate the same behavior.

DON'T SETTLE

I did. The older I got, the closer I followed in Mummy's footsteps. The way we are is not by accident. Most of our thoughts and behavior are learned from someone. My grandmother taught me that settling for anything people handed me was okay. This belief found its way not only in my intimate relationships, but all relationships. I became the punching bag for men to express their pain and the person people called when no one else was available.

It became normal for me to accept relationships I did not want because I did not grow up seeing anyone standing up for themselves. A part of me felt undeserving of love and prosperity. When I was a child my dreams were enormous and they lived inside of me. I always knew my place in the world was never quiet and contained. My mouth had speakers and my heart was an ocean filled with treasures. What was on the inside of me was greater than time and space. I believe all of us have felt the immense presence of God inside when we were children.

We were fearless and free, uninhibited and unique, however, somewhere along the journey of life someone or something taught us that we should all be the same. We should dress the same, think the same, and strive for the same thing. We lose our authenticity. We lose our power, and ultimately our spiritual design.

Beautiful, let us not repeat the mistake like the children of Israel and settle for a golden calf when we can abide in the presence and promises of God. No matter how many promises God has made, they are *"Yes in Christ."* 2 Corinthians 1:20. May we not allow our bad experiences in the past be the filter we use to decide who we are and what we will accept in our lives. Let us not wander in the dessert another year when our "promised land" is mere moments away. God is outside of the boxes into which we place ourselves. He is limitless and has a great plan for our lives. Settling should never be an option. Keep walking the walk of faith knowing within us is something precious and valuable to the Master. No matter what you have been through or where you have come from, you are always worth the wait.

Don't settle.

CHAPTER 4

PLAYING ON THE DEVIL'S PLAYGROUND

THE LITTLE BROWN girls dancing in a ring at lunchtime were expected to have good grades. Education was our way out of the slums and every grade above a C made our future more promising. Although I was one of the top students in my class, the classroom felt like a prison. The playground was where I felt most alive. It represented creativity and adventure. The playground, like art, morphed into whatever we wanted it to be. However, every now and then something would happen on the playground where someone fell, scraped their knee, or got into a fight because another child took the game too seriously.

We all stopped and paid attention to what caused the fun to come to a halt. Just like the schoolyard playground, the world we live in is one huge playground. At some point in our lives, we too will be thrown off course by the unexpected. We will fall, get wounded, or get in a wrestling match with evil. We become aware that the playground and the people we are playing with are not always playing the same game we are. Just like the fight, we are taken unawares and soon knocked to the ground.

At six years old everything changed one Thursday evening after school. It was just a normal evening, except this particular day, Mummy was frying chicken. Normally the menu would be fried escovitch red snapper, but Mummy believed she had figured out Colonel Sanders' secret to Kentucky Fried Chicken.

While she dipped chicken legs in the seasoned flour, I ran around the yard with my one-wheel cart several times. The third time around the compound, I stopped to see who had pulled up in a white 1980s Volkswagen Beetle in front of our gate. We were not expecting company. The car door opened and a very clean-shaven man in a white t-shirt and blue jeans stepped out of the car. He looked familiar, as if we had met somewhere. He was tall, with a small fade afro, and in his hand was the hugest doll I had ever seen. The longer I stared at him, I realized it was the same man in the photograph I hid in that old English dresser drawer. Clinging to his arm like a prize was a fair-skinned woman I had never seen before.

He took a step closer to the gate and called my name. I did not know whether to run to him, scream, or faint. My blue t-shirt was stained and my hair was a hot mess. I wished I was more prepared for his coming. Instead of running towards him, I dashed through the house into the kitchen to get Mummy.

"Daddy is at the gate!" I screamed.

"Jozanne, your father is not here," she replied. I tugged her skirt, loosening the string that held it up.

"Child, get off me and let me fry this chicken."

"Daddy is here! I said, jumping up and down.

She peered through the kitchen window and her jaw dropped as if she had seen a ghost.

"It's your father alright."

Immediately Mummy turned off the stove, ran to the closet, and removed her shirt, stained with grease. "He has the nerve showing up here five years later," she vented while searching through the closet, quickly throwing on her blue floral blouse she normally wore when she was about to meet someone of importance.

"Three weeks! Three weeks my behind. I will show him three weeks," she muttered.

It didn't matter why she was vexed with him, Daddy was *here*.

"Pass the face powder," Mummy said while placing a fake mole on her chin. She dabbed her face with loose powder and we both stared in the mirror for a split second before making our entrance out the front door.

When we came out, my father and the woman on his arm still stood there, picture perfect. Sashaying down the steps with her lips pouted, Mummy said, "Oh, so you finally made it back to Jamaica."

"I am here to see my daughter," my father replied with an American twang.

"This is Michelle, my fiancé," he said of the woman standing beside him. She flaunted the shiny diamond ring on her left hand. Mummy seemed annoyed by her presence, but I was mesmerized by them.

Dad stepped towards me and handed me the doll that had "Rosemarie" embroidered on the front of her dress. "Your Auntie Rosie wanted me to give this to you." Rosemarie's glass eyes were brown and her hair was just like mine, bushy and coarse. She had thick legs with a smooth chocolate caramel skin. I held Rosemarie, enamored by my father's presence.

His eyes were nothing like Jean's. With outstretched arms, he picked me up and hugged me. I lay there enveloped in his tight embrace and knew I found the place I belonged.

"I missed you, Daddy," I whispered in his ear.

"I missed you too," he whispered back. It was the first time a man hugged me, and being that it was my father, it lifted the shame I felt from Jean and Smith. My father had shown up and it gave me hope.

PLAYING ON THE DEVIL'S PLAYGROUND

YOU SHOWED UP

You showed up
The extra breath to my finish line.
My last name was no longer foreign
It found life in you
You showed up
And gave me a dream
I belonged
I was not a bastard and you were not a deadbeat.
You showed up
An empty cup and you filled my joy to the brim.
Bells rang and my heart danced
You showed up.

The dream was real and it was sealed with the smell of America on his clothes. That summer, with my head held high and my chest lifted up like a little peacock, we paraded through the neighborhood.

"This is my father. He came from America. He bought me Bazookas, Now and Laters, and Wrigley's. Do you want some?"

As I bragged to all the little girls in town, those three pieces of candy in my hand were like gold nuggets. They were made in America and I was a tiny step closer to the land of dreams and opportunity.

That summer Dad took me to visit his blind mother who lived only a few miles away. A heavyset dark-skinned woman sat in a living room full with figurines and smelled like baby powder. We had the same features; high cheekbones, wide noses, and full lips.

"Mom, guess who I brought with me?" my father said.

Clearing the phlegm from her throat, his mother said, "I hope it's your sister Rosie."

"No, it is your granddaughter, Jozanne."

"Jozanne! Come here child," she commanded. While I stood in front of her, she felt for my face, cuddling it with her hands. I could not resist grabbing a few of the candies placed in the dish on the table beside her and stuffing the sweets into my pocket.

"I see you like candy. Child, I am blind, not deaf," she said.

Then she reached over to the dish, handed me a few more, and gestured with her finger over her lips to keep it a secret from my father.

"Henry, why don't you get the girl some coconut ice cream," she beckoned to Dad in the kitchen.

Dad and I left the kitchen and made our way to relax in the back-yard. After a few licks of our coconut ice cream, he reached into his back pocket and from his wallet he pulled out an American five dollar bill and handed it to me. "Here you go, Jozanne. Buy whatever you want." I snatched the money from his hand. It was crisp and smelled as if it came right off the mint.

I jumped up on his lap and laid my head against his chest.

"I love you, Daddy." It was the first time I'd uttered those words to anyone. My emotions were raw and I wasn't sure if he felt the same way.

"How much do you love me?" he asked playfully.

I stretched my hands out as wide as I could. "Dis much."

Amused by my playfulness he said, "Give Daddy a kiss." I planted a big smack on his cheek.

"Give me another kiss," he said, and I planted another one on his cheek. He pulled my face towards him and kissed me on the lips. His tongue felt slimy and slippery like a worm.

"Daddy, that is nasty! You pushed your tongue in my mouth!" I screeched playfully.

Covering my mouth with his hands, he told me, "That is because you are beautiful, Jozanne."

Beautiful. Snow White is beautiful. Jessica in English class is beautiful. Princess Diana is beautiful. My name and *beautiful* in the same sentence was headline news, and because it came from my dad, it was now valid. The yucky snake in my mouth was no longer a factor. His celebration of me carried a greater weight. Maybe that was what daddies did, after all, this was the first time a male figure showed me any physical affection. Saying "I love you," hugging, and kissing the opposite sex was all new to me. Although his action felt weird, being beautiful in my father's eyes meant everything.

It meant I did not have to ask another soul for their approval. It meant acceptance of myself and how I showed up from that point. Not for one moment did I associate my experience with pain and fear.

The majority of times when children are molested, they are confused because they don't understand the difference. All they comprehend is the affection and affirmation they receive from the person they trust and admire.

The evening came to an end and it was time to head home. When Daddy dropped me off at the house, Mummy was already waiting at the gate with her hands on her hips. I couldn't wait to share the good news.

"Daddy told me I am *beautiful*, Mummy!"

"Good," she replied calmly.

"I am beautiful, Mummy. I am *beautiful!*"

It was more than "good." It was fantastic! It was life-changing. I had five American dollars and my father thought I was *beautiful*. Most little dark-skinned girls didn't get these kinds of compliments in our small town. Light-skinned girls were beautiful, not us. We were either admired for being smart, running track, or belting out a high note in the choir. This was as far the compliments went. My father's kiss was tucked in my heart and being *beautiful* stood at the forefront of my mind.

That night in my corner of the bed I reminisced on the entire day but didn't know what to make of this unusual kiss. After all, there was nothing to compare it to. This kind of affection was unfamiliar, yet I felt beautiful and that was all that mattered.

BEAUTIFUL

PLAYING ON THE DEVILS PLAYGROUND

I felt beautiful playing on the devil's playground
Where hide and seek was not the game
Secrets tucked away in my bosom
Love awakened so soon
In one afternoon
Went from two pigtails to a ponytail
The blush from my cheeks rushed from my lips
My innocence flew away from my lips
Confused why my heart was beating so fast
Embarrassed I laughed my shame away
I needed a hug.
I needed your love
I needed you
I felt beautiful playing on the devil's playground.

Dad's visit came to an end and the thought of him leaving me behind made me angry. Life was difficult for all of us and another five years without his presence would be unbearable. The day he was heading to the airport he stopped by with more coconut ice cream and a bag full of Wrigley's.

"I want to live with you," I told him.

"As soon as you get a visa," he promised. He handed Mummy cash, kissed me on the forehead, and drove away.

Smith, Mummy, and I watched from the gate until his cab disappeared around the corner. The clock had struck midnight and Cinderella had lost her glass slippers. We were back to our routine. Smith headed inside the house and poured himself a glass of Pepsi with some rum, while Mummy and I sat on the steps until the streetlights came on.

PLAYING ON THE DEVIL'S PLAYGROUND

I sat there wondering when I would see my father again. I was only six, and life was like an enormous jigsaw puzzle. My place in the world was lost in a fog of unanswered questions combined with a kiss that awakened a part of me I was too young to comprehend.

THE THIEF

The thief comes in the night
When all men's eyes are blinded by love
He takes stuff
He takes stuff
Stuff more precious than gold.
To him it's sweet, this stolen treat.
Tricked by a sugar coated tongue
He makes you think you are the only one.

The thief comes in the night
When all men's eyes are blinded by love
He takes stuff
He takes stuff
Stuff too deep to utter
It makes your heart flutter
The fox as cunning as a snake
You keep an oath for his namesake

The thief comes in the night
When all men's eyes are blinded by love
He takes stuff
He takes stuff

BEAUTIFUL

Call them secrets
It gives him power
The thief is closer than a friend
He keeps you silent until the end.

The thief comes in the night
When all men's eyes are blinded by love.

"Yearly, 6.6 million children are referred to child protection services, and 3.2 million of those children are subjected to an investigated report," says Child Help Organization. In one study, 80 percent of twenty-one-year-olds who reported childhood abuse met the criteria for one or more disorders, such as illicit drug abuse, depression, suicide attempts, and promiscuity.

Child abuse has no color. It's not a Black or White issue. Every race and culture has come face to face with this horrible issue. It takes place in homes, schools, and religious institutions. The unfortunate truth is that someone will encounter this horrible situation. It is even more painful when it comes from a family member.

Family wounds tend to linger deeper inside of us long after the deeds are done. They are the most stubborn problems to get rid of, especially when it is caused by a father or a mother. If a stranger breaks into our house unexpectedly we can make sense of it, but if the thief in the night lives in our household, it becomes harder to accept and recover from. When a father figure abuses a child it cripples that child's self-worth, which oftentimes leaves the child open prey to other perpetrators, and silence will be the response.

Our first experience of intimacy is vital in shaping our views of love and sex. Once love is corrupted, we spend our entire lives chasing the minion who perverted our conscience and lied to us that agape love never existed in the first place. My first kiss crossed boundaries and I was not brave enough to defend myself. These blurred lines left me questioning my good judgment. Many times children are not conscious of their abuse; especially if it was done in a subtle way. They might feel uncomfortable, but don't know how to articulate it. Silence is always the result.

Our uncertainty becomes a silence that roars with blame and shame on the inside, and as time goes by it becomes easier to move on with our lives without addressing it. Our violation goes acknowledged, and even when it's spoken there is no apology from the perpetrator or the people to whom we disclose our secrets.

My Prince Charming had shown up, but his charm came with a sting that later would poison my soul and change my view about men, and ultimately about God. A good father represents a good god. A father's presence and response to his daughter shapes her journey into womanhood, and every man she meets after him will subconsciously remind her of what is expected in a relationship. Women tend to gravitate to men who remind them of their fathers or try to find a father in the men they date. If our fathers are hard workers, we will be drawn to men who are ambitious. If he was an abuser, we tend to settle for men who are controlling and manipulative. Pediatrician Meg Meeker in her book *Strong Fathers, Strong Daughters: The 3 Day Challenge* describes fathers as *"a template for all male figures—teachers, boyfriends, husbands, uncles, and even God himself—in a daughter's life."* This shows how much influence a father plays in a daughter's life.

Child sexual abuse is often hidden. It's deceptive and manipulative. It seduces and conquers. It gets its life through the silence of its victim. The longer the victim plays the game of silence, the more it reigns. *"Yearly, almost 60,000 children are sexually abused in the United States alone. More than 90% of juvenile sexual abuse victims know their perpetrator,"* reports the Child Maltreatment Report. *"Child abuse crosses all socioeconomic and educational levels, religions, ethnic, and cultural groups."*

Unfortunately, the majority of these victims don't get the justice they deserve. They live in silence, and in shame, afraid to confront their perpetrator, much less disclose the violation. There are no apologies, only accusations, ridicule, and isolation.

Today, I would love to take this opportunity to say to you if you were ever violated, "I am sorry." I am sorry for everyone who unlawfully entered the gate of your soul and stole love. I apologize for every man or woman who has touched you inappropriately and left you confused and defenseless. I am sorry that you had to endure the burden of their secrets and shame when all you wanted to be was a child. I am deeply sorry for the tears it has caused you behind closed doors and the addictions it has created. You are not alone. I identify with your pain. But no other person feels the agony of our loss like Christ. Trust me, God shares in our suffering. Every affliction we have encountered breaks His heart. The enemy might be on the playground of our lives, ready to cause havoc, but like the teachers who are the watchmen on the playground to intervene when something goes wrong, so do we have an advocate to intercede on our behalf when the game is played unfairly. God is ready to step in and grant us justice. While it is difficult to acknowledge His presence when we have been taken advantage of, just because we don't see Him or feel Him does not mean He is not there.

Sometimes our wounds are so deep we are afraid to feel the gentle touch of the master's hands. We find ourselves running in the other direction. Unlike our abusers, however, His touch is pure, gentle, and filled with love. God is a giver, not a taker. He is the antithesis of all we experience with our abusers. He weeps over us and with us. He sees the dark things, even when it's done in secret. He is sensitive to the most secretive and sensitive details of our lives. He is the Ancient of Days, which means nothing under the sun goes unnoticed and hidden from the eyes of God. The young girl raped and buried out in the middle of nowhere is not forgotten. Her perpetrator might not be caught or prosecuted and we feel there is no justice, but one day, whether in the flesh or out of the body, justice will be served.

God knows and feels our deepest pain. Talk to him tonight. He is a confidante and a trusted friend. He longs to warm our hearts with compassion. Talk as long as you need. *"His ears are attentive to your cry."* Psalms 34:15.

No matter what happened in our lives, *"He who began a good work in you will finish it indefinitely in Christ Jesus."* Philippians 1:6. There is nothing impossible for God to accomplish in our lives. So many times we limit God to our own measure of faith. We see Him as we see those who have disappointed us and hurt us. But truth be told, God is different from the people we have experienced in our past. We must not relate to God through the lenses of our experiences. *"For God is not a man that He should lie."* Numbers 23:19.

He is the Great Physician of our souls, well capable to heal and set us free. He is infallible and a keeper of his word. Since His word is rooted in flawless love, it is unlike His nature to call a bluff in the midst of our own frailty. When we give God a chance to restore us we enter back to the garden of truth and experience the author of love. *"Because His loving-kindness is better than life."* Psalms 63:3. No matter the pain, He is waiting to restore, redeem, and have a new relationship with our hearts.

The world is our playground, a place in the universe designed for us to discover ourselves, carry out God's purpose, and be a blessing to others. Yet in this game called life it is inevitable that we all will encounter trials and tragedy. Still, these misfortunes do not have to be final. We get bruised and banged up by all kinds of situations and eventually we don't want to play again. We end up hiding from others and from ourselves. Out of shame we decide not to show up. Nevertheless, it's in brokenness that God gets most of His glory. It's there conquerors are made and warriors are born. It is in the dark places light shines the best. When we decide to show up regardless of what happened to us, God manifests his glory. If you have not shown up in your life, this is the time. It is your time to get up and come out on life's playground.

It's time to play again.

CHAPTER 5

SHE CRAZY

"Every year about 42.5 million American adults (or 18.2 percent of the total adult population in the United States) suffers from some mental illness, enduring conditions such as depression, bipolar disorder, or schizophrenia." (Newsweek)

"African Americans are 20% more likely to experience serious mental health problems than the general population," says the National Alliance of Mental Illness. Based on my experience, among Black culture mental illness becomes a conversation that we rarely discuss due to shame. Culturally we are expected to be strong and more resilient when it comes to depression and misfortune. Those who struggle with some form of psychological problems are normally shunned or ostracized.

"The most commonly diagnosed mental illnesses in Jamaica are depression and schizophrenia. The rates of depression are in line with global trends; a 2008 survey of the island found that 25.6 percent of females and 14.8 percent of males displayed symptoms of the condition. Neuropsychiatric disorders contribute an estimated twenty percent of the global burden of disease (2008)." (Commonwealth Health)

Growing up with a mother diagnosed as schizophrenic created deep shame. Being uneducated about these types of issues, the only way our family dealt with it was to keep silent. No one wanted to be embarrassed or even be associated with anyone who had a mental problem. It was considered demonic. The "crazy woman" or "crazy man" we saw on the street was trapped by a demon and we needed to stay clear. When it is a family member, it becomes a reality that we can't avoid or ignore. Despite common belief and superstition, having a mentally ill family member breaks our hearts. The helplessness devastates everyone and eventually we prefer not to talk about it. Soon they become strangers, often forgotten.

However, Mummy was not going to forget her daughter Jean. She was adamant about getting Jean out of the hospital, and every evening she hinted that if Jean was on the best behavior for nine months, the doctors would allow her to come home for a trial visit over the weekend. Well, Jean made it through the nine months and she was coming home for the weekend.

Smith wanted no part of it.

"She is my only daughter and I will not leave her in the hospital to die. She is coming home next week," Mummy firmly told him.

"She is crazy, Dixon."

"You are the crazy one, Smith, if you think I am not bringing my daughter home."

That week Smith drank like a sailor and they fought nightly about Mummy's final decision. The day before Jean's visit, Mummy spent the entire day cleaning, replacing the curtains, decorating the dining table, and preparing Jean's favorite stew peas and rice. It was a sleepless night for everyone. I had planned to jump through the bedroom window just in case Jean acted crazy or pretended to be dead the minute she start pounding on me.

Friday afternoon was upon us. Smith, my doll Rosemarie, and I waited on the verandah for their arrival, our nerves on high alert. The taxi pulled up and Jean stepped out, well-groomed in a blue and yellow floral dress. Mummy untied the chains from around the gate and escorted Jean into the house. I watched her walk up the steps in the most elegant fashion. I didn't know whether to run to embrace her or hide. So I sat there.

"Hi, Jossy," she said calmly.

"Say hello, Jozanne," Mummy prompted.

"Hello, Jean," I mumbled reluctantly. I didn't trust her.

We all went inside the house. The table was set with Mummy's best china as if we were expecting the Prime Minister of Jamaica. Mummy laid out dishes of curried chicken, stew peas, rice, green beans, freshly made carrot juice, and a few bottles of kola champagne. Smith made himself a plate and carried it to the verandah as usual. The clatter of forks against the plates was the only sound at the dinner table. I pushed my green beans from one side of the plate to another just to ease the tension.

"You betta eat those beans, Jozanne," Mummy scolded.

"Beans are good for you, Jossy. They will make you strong," Jean added.

I shoved a spoonful of beans in my mouth, excused myself from the table, and jumped onto the bed. Mummy gave me one of those "don't let me get the belt" looks but she kept her mouth closed. The tension was high and no one wanted to do or say anything to upset Jean. From the bed I watched Mummy's face light up like a Christmas tree. It was the happiest I had seen her in a long time. Like two old girlfriends catching up on lost times, Mummy and Jean chatted way past bedtime about when Jean was a little girl. I lay there staring at the ceiling until Mummy and Jean climbed into bed. There was not enough space on the bed for three, much less four. Smith already had a plan. He sat on a chair in front of the bed like a security guard with a piece of plywood in his hand. The three of us squeezed together on the bed, packed like sardines.

"Jean, you mek a move in dis house yu wi see who crazy in here tonight," Smith threatened. We all lay there on our backs, staring at the ceiling, waiting for Jean's time bomb to tick but she was fast asleep. Needless to say, no one else shut an eye the entire night.

Before the cock crowed on Saturday morning, Jean got dressed, cleaned the house, and volunteered to make cornmeal porridge. Still in bed, Mummy glowed with extreme pride that her prized possession was home. We ate the cornmeal porridge Jean made, and even Smith joined in. God was surely performing a miracle in front of our eyes.

SHE CRAZY

Since it was Saturday, our routine was to go downtown to the market and buy groceries for the week. That afternoon Mummy left Jean and Smith at home, but the entire night had made me extremely anxious. I fainted on top of one of the market women's yams. Mummy told me some of the vendors rushed over and poured water on my face while holding a damped napkin with rum over my nose. I am not sure if this was all true, because Jamaicans can embellish a story. Yet, it would not surprise me.

The crocus bag had beef neck bones, pumpkin, thyme, scotch bonnet peppers, and some yellow yams for the beef soup Mummy planned on making that evening. Once we were home, Jean helped knead the flour mixed with cornmeal for the dumplings. I mean come on, what good is beef soup without dumplings?

The soup was ready, hot with pepper and the healing smell of thyme. It was time to chow down in the ninety-five-degree heat. This was the first time we all sat down together to eat as a family. After dinner was over I retreated under the huge Saint Julian mango tree to read my nursery rhymes.

After a while, Jean walked over and sat beside me. "Read me your nursery rhyme, Jossy," she said. Her eyes were welcoming, her spirit cool as a cucumber. It was the first time I saw my mother "normal."

"I want to hear your nursery rhymes, Jossy," she persisted.

"Which one?"

"Any one."

"Little Miss Muffet?"

"Yes, read that one."

I jumped up, tied a knot in my shirt, and went on to perform "Little Miss Muffet." Jean was tickled pink by my performance, laughing until her stomach was in knots. It was delightful to see her pearly white teeth, mahogany skin, and long, curly hair. I was a little too dramatic just about everything. Mummy always told me that God is passionate, so make sure I do everything with excellence. Well, *Little Miss Muffet* was now an off-Broadway production. Maybe God did answer Mummy's prayer after all. That evening I performed from *Old Mother Hubbard, Jack and Jill,* and *Twinkle Twinkle Star.* I read my mother every nursery rhyme in my book that day.

Around six o'clock, Smith headed back to work at the airport and once again the three of us gathered on the front porch talking about every and anything. Jean turned to me and said, "Jossy, when you grow up, be a good girl, you hear? And stay away from men. Men will make you crazy." I did not know what to make of her statement so I just nodded in agreement.

The streetlights came on and it was time for bed, but Jean did not move, she stared at me from under her eyebrows the way she did the first time we met at Bellevue Hospital. I knew something was wrong because fear came over me. I got up, walked swiftly to the gate, and stood there. Jean got up from the steps and speedily walked towards me. I knew she was going to hurt me so I tried unwrapping the chain to get out but couldn't, so I climbed over the gate. Jean climbed behind me and I ran as fast as I could down the street, screaming on top of my voice, "Help!" The neighbors ran outside to see what the commotion was all about.

Jean was chasing me down the street, screaming and ripping her clothes off until she was completely naked. Mummy followed, trying to keep up. I ran to Mummy's friend's house banging and yelling, "Ms. Gracie! Ms. Gracie! Open the gate! Jean is going to kill me! She is going to kill Mummy too!"

Ms. Gracie stepped out of her house with a blunt in one hand and a Red Stripe beer in the other. "Calm down, child. No one is going to kill anybody."

"Yes, she will. Yes she will, Ms. Gracie!" I cried. Ms. Gracie opened the gate, beckoning her son, "Desmond, get this girl a popsicle, let mi see what a'gwan."

I did not want any popsicle. I wanted to know if Mummy was alive. Worried about her, I glanced down the street but she was nowhere in sight.

"Come inside, rude girl," Ms. Gracie said. I didn't. I sat there for the rest of the evening waiting for Mummy to show up. It was after dark when Mummy made it to Ms. Gracie's house. Too angry, I did not know whether to hug her or scream for making me worry. To make matters worse that evening, everyone in town heard the news about my mother, including all the little girls who went to school with me.

SHE CRAZY

She crazy
This gal stripping down to her private parts
Breaking her mother's heart
Running like she wild
Dis woman one child
She crazy
She crazy
Done lost her mind
Confined
Di father left dem behind
Where did she come from?
No one talked about her man

She Crazy
She Crazy

Three men restrained her
Everybody feared her
Her child made her crazy

BEAUTIFUL

Poor little baby
Too bad her mother is crazy
She Crazy
She Crazy

Three grown men restrained Jean in the square. My mother's nakedness was the talk of the town for months. The embarrassment, the gossip, the humiliation. The harder I tried to love her, the deeper I hated being her daughter. That night I spent the night at Ms. Gracie's house, coiled up on her couch that smelled like she had a thousand pounds of marijuana stuffed into it. That night on Ms. Gracie's couch I promised myself to never see Jean again.

There couldn't possibly be any beauty in all this chaos. Facing the little girls at school on Monday morning after lying about Jean being a flight attendant left me walking with my head in the sand. From that day I nagged Mummy daily, "Send me to America. I want to live with Daddy."

"It's not that easy, Jozanne."

"I want to go to America!"

"Your father is not that great either, Jozanne."

"Well at least he is not crazy."

"You hush your mouth right now!"

To me, my mother was to blame for all the pain we were going through. Eventually Mummy became sick of all the nagging and every Saturday evening we travelled into town to make collect calls to Dad at the payphone by Sal's Groceries and Tings. The constant fracas between them was obvious by the slamming down of phones. But I could of cared less about their squabble. I wanted to leave Jamaica.

Jean was admitted back to Bellevue and this time it didn't matter if she came home again. I had lost all hope that she would get better. For fifteen years I rarely talked about my mother and rarely did anyone ask. I became the motherless child. It's a conversation most people don't care to discuss, even those who are close to you. Victims of mental illness are often times forgotten and I got used to the silence that lurks behind this disease. Not talking about it does not make it disappear though. A young girl was locked away and ostracized by her family and only one person had the faith and courage to fight for her, but even Mummy got tired.

Like I shared before, mental illness is rarely discussed in the Black community. It's a strange phenomenon to many and to some it's "White people problems." The common response is, "What do you mean you have psychological problems? Be strong. Go to church. God will take care of it. Pray. Be happy. Girl, there is nothing to worry about. Stop thinking so hard." People of color are compelled to be strong, resilient, and overcome whatever hardship we encounter. However, according to the U. S Department of Health and Human Services, Office of Minority Service, African Americans are 20 percent more likely to report having serious psychological distress than non-Hispanic minorities and Whites.

Hiding our mentally ill family members does not help the situation, neither does locking them away in an institution make life any easier. So what do we do when a family member is mentally ill? How should we deal with it? We seek out ways for their healing and recovery. Emotional healing is a journey, not an event. It takes time seeking, searching, and praying in the secret place with the One who truly understands the complexities of our lives. God will guide our steps, grant us answers, and lead us to a place of peace. We might not always get the answer we desire but one thing I can assure is that peace will come. Mummy and Smith were too afraid to seek out an answer to the problem. Both of my guardians were on two opposite extremes. One obsessed about the outcome she wanted, and the other had completely given up on the possibility. Too often we equate peace with the outcome we want rather than letting the outcome give us peace. This life has questions unanswered and answers we don't understand. This is where faith comes in. Faith says, *I don't understand but I trust the One who knows all things.*

In a world served with chaos and pain, Jesus came to restore us back to peace. In physics, the law of thermodynamics is fascinating. The Law of Entropy talks about the world going from a state of order to disorder. For example, if we neatly place all our socks in a drawer, soon enough after a week, our socks drawer will be out of order and we will have to redo it. The world is constantly dissipating, no matter how we attempt to fix and bring order, something will happen that creates disorder and chaos.

Jesus came to bring order. In Him, the reverse of entropy happens, and all that was out of order comes back to its rightful place. Jesus is the Prince of Peace. This is what happens to our emotional wounds; God is able to restore us back before the beginning of time. In Psalms 23: 3, scripture says, *"He restores my soul."* To "restore" means to "bring back." In Hebrew it means, "Bring back to health." The word "soul" means the "nefesh" in Hebrew, which means "life." I am not saying it won't take any effort on our part. We must participate in our healing. The fact that we are being restored implies our original state was damaged.

We all have been damaged mentally in some ways, some more severe than others. We find ourselves out of our right minds. We behave irrationally and the only thing that can get us back to who we once were is love.

I love the way Jesus loves us. The power of God's love is transformative. We don't know their background of the majority of people Jesus delivered in the Bible, their specific age, or sometimes their religious outlook on life. Jesus' main focus was on solutions. His intention was to demonstrate love, grace, and mercy. He saw purpose in each life He touched. He loved on purpose, which ultimately gave His Heavenly Father all the glory. How can God get glory from our mentally challenged family members and peers? Love is the answer. We show up in the way they need us.

Ostracizing them is definitely not the answer. Demanding that they be the way we envision them can be overwhelming. Jesus' response to difficult situations teaches us not just about God's love, but His character as well.

First, Jesus did not ignore pain and turmoil, He addressed it. It doesn't matter how overwhelming the situation, there is always a solution. Avoidance and silence are normally our response to problems we find difficult to solve. Sometimes we don't know the solution to the problem but when we confront it, it stretches our faith and gives God the opportunity to move in a mighty way. Solutions come when we take steps of faith.

Second, it's important that we leave the outcome to God. Often we assume "this is the way we should go." When God does not respond the way we think He ought to, we become discouraged and feel like we have failed or God does not love us. God does not always answer us based on our expectations, he answers us based on His purpose. *"His ways are not our ways and His thoughts are not our thoughts."* Isaiah 55:8. Beautiful, there are some things in this life we will never have full understanding of.

I am not sure why things did not work out for my mother. What I *am* sure of is that every time I picked up the phone and called her, I restored her dignity. I placed a smile on her face. I let her know she had value and worth. The rest of her days were joyful and she lived in hope. It's not about how we think someone should be loved but what makes them *feel* loved is truly what matters. It's meeting them where they are and never about bringing them to where we are. The pressure to drive our own agenda in order to fulfill an outcome that looks like "God's will" can often times wrapped up in ego, pride, and self-righteousness.

These things will not allow us to enjoy the process and see the goodness of God in circumstances we don't understand. We end up living in a place of defeat and only seeing our lives through the lens of one incident. This is definitely a smoke screen to prevent us from really seeing the big picture. I talk about the *big picture* because too often we see our lives through a microscopic lens, ignoring the panoramic view of God's standpoint.

Once in a while I love going to the top of Runyon Canyon and looking out over the city. It reminds me that *my* plans for my life are teensy compared to God's worldview.

There came a point in my life where my torn relationship with my mother had an expiration date. She was in the hospital and there was nothing I could do about it. All that was required was me showing up where she needed me the most. She needed to hear my voice. She needed clothes, shoes, and food. She needed prayer. She needed to know how much I cared. She needed to know I loved her. She needed to be remembered. She needed support. I did not have the finances to buy her a home, take her around the world, or give her the best care as I hoped, but I gave her what she needed each day. I learned to give her out of my financial lack. I learned to love her out of my own disappointment and pain. I learned to listen even when I did not understand.

God is not always in the theatrics. He is found in the simple things we dismiss as mundane. That's where the magic happens. It is silent and hidden deep in the soul. The last few years of Jean's life we spoke more. Our conversations on the phone sometimes basked in the silence of unspoken needs. I wanted to give her the world but I *was* her world and did not know it. At her funeral, I learned more about Jean, the woman. She was not the crazy girl I grew up hearing about. She was storyteller. She told it like it was and stayed silent even if others were uncomfortable. She was a helper to all the other patients in the hospital. Jean loved reading scriptures and loved God. She laughed more than she cried. She never complained despite the situation she found herself in. She forgave those who offended her. She was remembered as a beacon of light.

Jean Maureen Ashley was also a mother. My mother. Although she never nurtured me per se, she taught me that sometimes while we are not always in the perfect situation, we can still discover beauty in the moments we have now. Jean loved me with all her heart. She spoke about me often. Jean lived not the way we desired, but lived her best life in her circumstances.

One of the stories I heard about my mother that brought me great joy was her taking care of a baby girl who was abandoned in the missions where she stayed the last four months of her life. The nuns shared about her love for this little girl. God had definitely healed her heart. This story stood out for many reasons, which I will discuss later.

Yes, my mother suffered from mental illness, but in her own unique way she exuded great love and lived a purpose way beyond the walls behind which she was confined. Looking through the lens of Heaven, Jean was not just a mentally ill woman; her life was wrapped up in the infallible wisdom of God.

Love will always transform others.

CHAPTER 6

SHAMEFUL THINGS

There is a Brown Girl in the Ring
Tra La la la la...
There is a Brown Girl in the Ring
Tra La la la la..."

DURING LUNCHTIME THE little brown skinned girls held hands in a circle while one girl danced in the middle. We loved the game "brown girl in the ring." Each little girl was unique, beautiful, unafraid, and unashamed. Our green and white plaid skirts swayed in the breeze as we cheered her on. There was no other like her at Saint George's Girls' School.

Our school was housed in an Anglican Church on Duke Street in downtown Kingston. Every parent wanted to send their little girls there, so they would grow up well educated, well-mannered, and stay pure. The teachers were extremely strict, especially our Chinese Jamaican English teacher Miss May. Whenever she went to a staff meeting, most of the little dark-skinned girls raised their hands to be classroom monitors. "Me, me, pick me, Miss May!" they yelled. Miss May always chose Jessica, the light-skinned girl with bone straight hair who sat dead center in the front row.

SHAMEFUL THINGS

It was obvious she had special privileges. She was always used as an example of poise and beauty. Soon enough we grew weary of combing our wooly hair and being in our brown skin didn't feel as beautiful. Jessica's caramel skin reminded every cocoa skinned girl she was not pretty enough or good enough.

It was not Jessica's fault. It was the way Miss May treated her with such honor that left us feeling inadequate.

One day Miss May left for a staff meeting. "Students, Jessica will be classroom monitor until I get back. Jessica, please report if any one acts uncivilized." We couldn't wait until Miss May left the classroom. Several students jumped out of their seat, singing and dancing on top of the tables.

Miss May. Miss May, nu come back today. Please, Miss May nu come back today."

Jessica begged for us to settle down but no one listened. My very rambunctious friend Lisa yanked me from my seat. "Come nuh, Jozanne. Dance wid us nuh."

"No man, mi nuh wan to get in a trouble."

"Jozanne, stop being a scaredy cat."

Of course I wanted to celebrate our freedom from the tyrant that ran first grade with an iron fist. I jumped on Miss May's desk and joined in the praise dance singing, "Miss May, Miss May, nu come back today. Please, Miss May, nu come back today."

I was standing on the desk with my eyes closed, gyrating my waist as the room cheered me on. Suddenly the students scattered to their seats and Miss May's shadow in front of me loomed ten feet tall from the classroom door behind me.

"Where would you like me to go, Jozanne?" she said with her hands on her hips and fire flaring from her nostrils. I quietly stepped down from the desk and walked to my seat.

Piqued, Miss May stormed over. "Did you hear me ask you a question?"

With a gritty smile on my face I said, "Miss May, we were just playing wid yu, man."

"Pick up your belongings and let's go play at the principal's office."

Going to Principal Miller's office was like receiving a death sentence. On the walk down the hallway I felt like Sean Penn in *Dead Man Walking*. Everyone knew I was about to get a whipping. Miss May entered the office and closed the door behind her. I stood outside of Miss Miller's door waiting and waiting while Miss May filed her complaint against me. Suddenly, the door swung open and Miss May strutted past me with a smirk on her face.

I barged into Miss Miller's office. If I was going down, everyone in class was going down with me. "Miss Miller! Miss Miller! I was not the only one out dere playing. Charmaine and Winsome and Ingrid was playing too!"

Behind the desk sat a Caucasian woman with the reddest cheeks ever from all the rouge she applied. Her hair was neatly kept in a bun perched on top of her head, and her round framed glasses sat perfectly on the tip of her nose. Poised and unaffected by my temper tantrum, she spoke calmly and sternly. "Were you told the rules, Jozanne?" I said nothing. "Speak child!" she said.

"Miss May, I was not the only one."

"Those who know better must do better."

She reached under her desk as if she was a villain from a James Bond movie who had a secret weapon of warfare hidden under there. "Lift up your skirt," she said.

Hesitantly, I lifted the hem of my skirt and positioned my bare leg.

With her long bamboo cane, she beat me on my leg over and over until it was completely numb. The students heard my hooting and hollering from down the hall as each strike came down with a vengeance. Miss Miller exhausted herself on my thigh, sweating and breathing hard. She was determined to beat the black off me.

"Go back to your class. Next time, you follow the rules," she scolded.

I did not budge.

"Do you want more, Jozanne?"

We stood there looking at each other. With a sinister scowl, she got real close to my face. The darkness of racism and discrimination echoed through her voice. "You go back to class or you will get another whipping," she threatened. I stood there. "Child, get back to class, *now*!"

The damage was already done.

There was no way I could return to class. I am not sure what had gotten into me, because I was not the kind of child to mouth off to an adult. The punishment was severe and we both knew it. Those lashes on my leg were more than a reprimand; they spoke hate, anger, and prejudice. That afternoon I walked off campus without any permission and headed home.

Mummy was surprised to see me home so early, upset when she heard of my disobedience, and livid when she saw the black and blue stripes on my leg. She hit the roof. "Miss Miller did this to you!

Come, let us go down to the school. We will see who give birth to you today!"

She was so angry she left in her housedress. By the time we arrived school had just let out and everyone knew if Miss Dixon was there in her housedress we had a problem.

Mummy grabbed me by the hand and barged into Miss Miller's office, uttering under her breath, "Jesus, don't let me kill this woman today."

Startled, Miss Miller jumped from her seat. "Ms. Dixon, you cannot enter my office without permission!"

Mummy had no time for the foolishness that day. "Jozanne, lift up your skirt," she ordered.

I was not sure who I should listen to since they both had the authority to give me a thrashing. Since I had to go back home with Mummy I chose wisely. I lifted my skirt to my waist, revealing the black and blue welts on my leg.

"Look at my granddaughter's leg," Mummy continued. "Do you have any children? No, right? Well, you don't have the right to beat my granddaughter until she can't walk. Where is dat Miss May!"

"Jozanne broke the rules," Miss Miller said in a smug and overly-proper voice.

Mummy made it very clear that the only rules broken were those of abuse and prejudice. She grabbed Miss Miller's cane from the desk, pointing it in her face. "Look, if you let dis cane even come within a foot of my granddaughter again I will break it on you. You feel me? Irie! As a matter of fact, take Jozanne out of Miss May's class as of Monday morning or you both will find yourselves in the unemployment line."

Miss Miller and I braced ourselves as Mummy waved the cane at us. Then Mummy marched over to me, still pointing the cane. "Jozanne, with God anything is possible," she said. "You are just as capable as any of these children in town despite the color of your skin." Then she turned to Miss Miller, broke the cane in half, and left it on her desk.

We exited Miss Miller's office like bosses. I remember the warm feeling that came over me. Justice, love, and freedom felt good. Mummy was like Moses; whatever she had in her hand parted the Red Seas. She was my freedom fighter, fighting wars from nine to five, and I wanted to be just like her.

From that day on the little brown skinned girls of Saint George's Girls' School were treated with respect and dignity. Although she probably could have handled it in a more civil manner, I do not disregard Mummy's bravery. She was my hero. Her showing up at school that day taught me never to let anyone take advantage of me or others because the works of God's hands were justice and truth, and it was worth fighting for even if you had to do it in your housedress.

YOU ARE ENOUGH

Who told you your skin color was a curse?
Who told you your greatness was limited?
Who told you were invisible?
Who told you?
Who told you your soul had no value?
Who told you, you had too much lips, too much hair?
Too much to change
Too much to care

Who told you your skin was a curse?
Who have you been talking to?
Black Girls
Who told you?
Who told you, you had no way out?
Who told you your dreams would stay just dreams?
Who told you you were lesser than?
Who told you, that you are a...
Nigger?
Ghetto?
Uneducated?
Ugly?
Unworthy?
Limited?
Insignificant?
Black Girls, who told you?

BEAUTIFUL

You are more than BLACK
You are more than a color
You are more than stereotypes
You are more than a cliché
You are...
Fearfully and wonderfully made
In the image of God
Light skinned, chocolate, caramel,
Thin, slim, big boned,
Bone straight, curly, nappy,
Black Girls,
You are ENOUGH
Been enough since the first day of creation
Enough since the ocean had water
Enough since the sun shined
Enough since the stars sparkled in the sky
Enough since Jesus walked on water
Enough from roach infested apartments to being your OWN.
Enough from cotton fields to Buckingham Palace
Enough from the underground railroad to 1600 Pennsylvania
Ave
Enough when we weren't a thought
Oh, Black Girl, you are enough.
YOU ARE ENOUGH

Saint George's Girls' School taught me the bravest act I will ever accomplish is being who God called me to be. At some point someone will try to take that from me. I needed to stand up for myself, unashamed and unafraid. Easier said than done. Shame was the villain I could not get rid of. Shame was always close by, waiting to devour me, reminding me that I was never going to be enough. If it couldn't get me publicly, shame would ravage me secretly.

It's nighttime and there I am walking in the middle of the street wearing only a shirt and my underwear. Other times I am fully naked. Everyone is staring and the overwhelming feeling of embarrassment overtakes me as pedestrians stare. There is no place to run or hide. All eyes are on me. Then I wake up.

This recurring dream always had me jumping out of my sleep in a cold sweat, fearful and humiliated.

Shame is a debilitating feeling mixed with guilt, regret, and dishonor, often leaving us in hiding and silence. Although everyone on the planet struggles with shame at one point or another, nothing can feel more shameful than when someone you trust violates you sexually. Our entire world turns upside down and inside out. The world as we knew it is now unsafe and unpredictable. Sexual violation stains our lives with unworthiness and self-loathing. It's an unforgettable moment, and just like in my dream, you feel like everyone is watching what occurred in the secret place. My father kissing me inappropriately was my first sexual encounter, and what followed not only left me ashamed, it left me traumatized.

Mummy had put Miss Miller in her place and life at Saint George's was liberating for all the little brown girls. Every one that semester knew my name, even Roy the kind and playful custodian. The little girls circled around him after school as he handed them lollipops or "suck suck," a combination of water and red syrup frozen in a plastic bag and we sucked on it. Pretty simple. This was our Jamaican Popsicle. No comments necessary. #icant

Roy made sure he had a popsicle for me every Thursday evening after school, during "Study Hall," an afterschool program for students to excel in their studies. Mummy heard of Roy's benevolence and left him in charge of me. This way I stayed out of trouble and focused on passing final exams.

One evening Roy asked me to accompany him across the street so he could keep an eye on me while he cleaned another school adjacent to ours. Seeing I was fascinated by the Walkman he carried on his hip, he handed it to me. "Here, listen to some music," he said. Delighted, I pranced around the yard listening to Jimmy Cliff. With his bucket and mop, gradually Roy made his way inside the boys' restroom while I waited by the door.

I stood close to the dingy bathroom door as he mopped the floor. Once in a while he looked up and smiled. Eventually this became our regular routine after school. There was nothing to be afraid of. One evening while I waited by the bathroom door, Roy asked, "Do you like me?"

Of course I liked him. What was there not to like? He was kind, funny, and Mummy trusted him.

"Can you do something for me?" he asked. "It will be our little secret."

"Okay," I told him.

Roy took my hand and ushered me into the restroom, then plops his genital in my hands, smiling. Trying to prevent him from knowing how repulsed I felt, I smiled back.

"Man, you are beautiful," he said. This was the second time a man was taking advantage of me and telling me I was beautiful all in the same sentence.

He wiped the semen from my hands with the cloth he used to clean the mirror and I bolted out of the bathroom, darted down the street, and to the bus station. The stench of him lingered with every step. Too ashamed to get on the bus just in case the passengers knew I did something wrong, I walked the entire way home. Not for a second did I think Roy was responsible for his actions. The entire way home I blamed myself for entering the bathroom. I blamed myself for listening to his Walkman. I blamed myself for saying, "Okay."

At the dinner table that evening, Mummy kept asking "Why are you not eating? Eat, you love hot dogs. What is wrong with you, Jozanne?"

"Nothing. I am not hungry."

"Are you sick?"

"No. I just want to go to bed."

"Did anyone make you upset at school today?"

"I just don't feel well."

It was difficult to bring myself to tell my grandmother the man she trusted took advantage of me. I did not want her going down to the school and making another scene, especially about this topic. I had already had my brush with shame and could not stand another episode of ridicule.

No amount of bathing got rid of Roy's odor. The memory lingered in my head and I hid the disgust I felt about myself. I could not eat another hot dog because it reminded me of him. At eight years old the men in my life were teaching me they were abusive, sneaky, and perverted. It was the first time I had ever seen a man exposed and it made me sick on the inside.

It all happened so fast without any time to think, breathe, or scream. Normally that's how most assaults happen. It surprises you in the weirdest places and with the most familiar people. A lot of times children are assaulted right in front of our eyes and we don't see it. Trust is built and it blinds us from believing that a trustworthy person would betray you in such a way.

The once lively playground became a cemetery where innocence was buried beneath its Christian façade and the green and white plaid uniforms lost their honor. A piece of my soul was buried in the boys' bathroom across the street and my hands were smeared by perversion, manipulation, and betrayal.

After school was no longer fun. Most evenings with my face pressed against the fence as I watched Roy befriend other little girls, I felt even more helpless. They were his next victims. We never spoke to each other again. My voice was trapped on the inside of me like a prisoner. My thoughts played both defendant and prosecutor at the same time. Who do we tell these secrets to? Who believes the child? Why would anyone believe that the charming, friendly custodian who had worked several years at the school was a pedophile? After all, no other child had come forth. No one wants to be the first to expose the perpetrator. No one wants to be the bad guy.

Whenever we find ourselves in situations that leave us feeling dirty on the inside, remember God has the power to consecrate whatever was desecrated. Everything that causes us harm matters to the Him. *"And may you have the power to understand, as all God's people should, how wide, how long, how high, and how deep His love is."* Ephesians 3:18. Sometimes, the dilemma is we don't believe God's love can reach the shameful places. It seems overwhelming, dark, and embarrassing. As a result, we conceal our shame and suffer emotionally in silence.

Since advocating for women through the Beautiful Campaign, I have come across women who think rape is not a big deal. One family member stated, "Why couldn't the man marry the woman after raping her? This kind of thing happens in my country all the time. Just move on." Another woman said, "If you are molested by a family member, keep it to yourself. Family sticks together no matter what." I even came across a man who had the same point of view when it came to rape. "It's your family, why would you hurt them that way?"

Notice no one considers the victim. The victim becomes silent and invisible all over again. When we ignore or dismiss victims of abuse, we ultimately convey to them, "We don't want to hear how you feel." "No one cares." "Be quiet, you are a troublemaker." Although it is not verbal, these actions keep the victim at a distance and sooner or later they start believing it really does not matter.

"Just move on." No one cares.

It is this kind of thinking that has kept us still advocating for domestic violence and sexual assault. No one has the right to violate another human being. *"Do what is just and right. Rescue from the hand of the oppressor the one who has been robbed. Do no wrong or violence to the foreigner, the fatherless, or the widow, and do not shed innocent blood in this place."* Jeremiah 22:3. The nature of God is one of justice. We can't say we believe in a good and loving God and not stand up for those who are innocent, helpless, and voiceless.

Love is an action word and it demands us to go the extra mile for someone. Love provokes our spirit to do the right thing. Love never stays silent when anyone is taken advantage of. Love insists that the truth be held up like a banner. It will march for one. It will die for one. Jesus Christ knew we would encounter misplaced shame and that is one of the reasons he went to the cross. He himself was taken advantage of and beaten through the streets of Jerusalem for no particular reason. Think of the shame He must have felt being ridiculed, beaten, and stripped almost naked. People spat in his face and cursed at him. His only crime was love. His only crime was He knew who he was and his assignment on this Earth.

Jesus understands shame to its core, yet He reminds us that we have the ability to trust in the promises that God is able to raise us up from the pits of shame and declare us victorious. Not only can we rise from shame, He has given us power over it.

Every violation matters to God, even if this savage act was committed against us for the hundredth time and hundreds of years ago. He is the "Ancient of Days,' which means He sees all things and will judge and vindicate those who are innocent, whether in this world or the one unseen. Whatever was done in the dark will be shown in the light.

If you have experienced similar situations, remember the shame does not belong to you. We are not responsible for our perpetrators' feelings or sexual misconduct, no matter the deceit, the violence, or the shame that has taken place in our lives. *"No one who believes in the Lord shall be put to shame."* Romans 10:11. Every pain and shame suffered matters to our loving Father. Sometimes we brush off our shameful experiences thinking *at least my situation was not as bad as someone else's.* But it does matter.

Once a seed of corruption is planted in our souls, if it is not uprooted and replaced with the incorruptible word of God, these seeds eventually decay our soul. When someone commits the act of rape, they have not only violated the person intimately, they have caused damage to their soul, pervert love, and incur spiritual death not just to the victim, but everyone who encounters that person thereafter.

God's creation was not meant to harm to one another. We were supposed to be the patent image of His character and nature, which is to love deeply. God's image is filled with pure light and in Him there is no darkness at all.

We all have free will to walk in the Light or in Darkness. To every man on the face of this earth, we are given a choice whether to be led by the flesh or the Spirit. And to be in the Spirit yielding to God is necessary. For there are times when our hearts betray us and we are no longer compelled by love but by our fleshly desires. This is such a difficult concept for people to grasp because of our definition of "good." Scripture tells us, *"The heart of man is deceitful and desperately wicked, who can know it?"* Jeremiah 17:9. It is not only our actions that declare us "good," but the disposition of our hearts. The word "good" in Hebrew means flawless or perfect.

Our hearts outside of the Spirit of God are fragile, double minded, and capable of yielding to darkness. To have another human being commit an act of violence can cause much damage if we don't seek healing and restoration.

Ignoring Roy's action, I later developed feelings of unworthiness and rage. Anyone who violates us sexually is violent. They may not have held us down on a bed and force themselves on us, but they manipulated our minds and took advantage of our trust.

Roy's destructive act left unattended produced fruits of fear and shame in my own personal life. My spiritual immune system was now exposed and vulnerable to everything that was toxic for my soul. It was the first time I understood that I was being molested, yet it was difficult to speak to anyone about this private and shameful incident.

SHAMEFUL THINGS

Most families avoid talking about molestation even when they know it is happening. The fear sets in for everyone. No one wants to be associated with the shame it carries. Keeping our mouths closed will not solve the issue, nor will blaming the child clear our consciences. Change will never come until we are willing to deal with it. If child molestation is not addressed, the victim suffers greatly and the after effects become deeper as the individual matures.

It is stated that infancy to six years old is when the child is more observant, receptive, and their character is being built. We all know there are childhood behaviors we take along with us right into our adult years. While some of these habits are admirable, there are things we perceive and experience as children that leave an ugly impression on us. Later in our adult years they are manifested. If we grow up in a house where we have a loving father and/or mother, we will automatically want to be just like them when we become parents. Whatever we experience as children stays with us. Here I am in my thirties and I still love cooking everything with onions and tomatoes. Why? My grandmother, no matter what she was cooking, onions and tomatoes was the main ingredient. The way we handle our childhood trauma ultimately leaves an imprint on our hearts as we move forward with our lives.

I can see it right now. Your stomach is turning on the inside and you probably prefer to close the pages of this book right now and pretend you have not heard what you've read so far. If this applies to you, my sweet friend, I totally understand. But you are not alone. We all have deep secrets we are ashamed of. My past secrets had left me paralyzed in some areas of my life for many years. It walked with me into churches, auditions, and even in my friendships. Although I knew scriptures, went to church, and knew the right things to say, shame accompanied me everywhere.

We must come to a point where we no longer allow shame to rob us of destiny and identity. Shame is always there to steal our joy and keep us silent. It will ransack our emotions and leave us incapable of moving forward. One of the greatest weapons against shame is breaking the silence and declaring the truth about who God says we are.

Our tongue was created to declare the goodness of God and establish His truth over our lives. Once I knew God had given me the authority to utter goodness and truth in my circumstances, I began sharing with close friends about my molestation. I sat many days in a guidance counselor's office and cried. I prayed, I confessed, I became intentional about my restoration to wholeness and whatever it took, I was going to do. Shame was my Jericho and I walked around its walls for years, declaring it will not have power over me and one day it all came crashing down. Hence this book.

Beautiful, someone might have violated you and left you feeling insecure, foolish, unworthy, and shameful. Anger has taken root because of your silence, but today you can start with a whisper. Declare your freedom. You have negatively judged yourself for too long. This toxicity might have left you paralyzed, but you do not have to be ruled by shameful things. Do not spend another day allowing shame to rob you of love, joy, and relationship with others.

It's time to throw out the scripted dialogue that polices your freedom and imprisons your identity. Let's cultivate some new conversations with ourselves. As a psychology major in college, it was taught to us that engaging in new thoughts and behaviors daily increase the nerve connections in our brain.

Here are three things that helped me along the way…

I read specific scriptures that affirmed me daily. It made me less responsive to the old thoughts of unworthiness. Read books that inspire you. Write out inspirational quotes that give your soul life and say them every morning. When you continually hear and speak these things, they will manifest on the inside of you.

I became compassionate and gentle with myself. We all tend to be harsh with ourselves. The gentler I became with my healing and pain, the more peace guarded my heart against the anger I felt from never speaking up earlier. I also learned to accept a compliment. Instead of rejecting compliments, I kindly now say, "Thank you."

I forgave the people who harmed me. Forgiveness is a huge component for healing sexual trauma. I will discuss this in further chapters. Without forgiveness, we forfeit wholeness.

Beautiful, God has given you the keys to change the narrative for your life. He is capable of healing the shameful places of our lives. *"Instead of their shame my people will receive a double portion, and instead of disgrace they will rejoice in their inheritance; and so they will inherit a double portion in their land, and everlasting joy will be theirs."* Isaiah 61:7.

No matter how broken we are from sexual abuse, with prayer and the power of the Holy Spirit, God is more than able to restore our ashes to beauty. Grab hold of freedom, relinquish the past, embrace the love of healthy relationships, and bask in the presence of a loving God that sees us as shameless.

Be unashamed and unafraid.

CHAPTER 7

NO GOLD STREETS

My RAMBUNCTIOUS FRIEND Lisa and I spent many days sitting on the stairs at break time daydreaming about the day our feet touched the ground in America. America was where dreams came true. The streets were paved with gold and you could buy anything for ninety-nine cents. That was what our parents told us. Every little Jamaican girl wanted to walk those gold streets.

I had a fifty percent chance of living in the United States since my father lived there. Many nights lying in bed while Smith worked at the airport, I questioned Mummy about those streets. I wanted to be an American. America was associated with happiness, wealth, and prosperity. Mummy finally nagged my father enough to make him file for my visa. Month after month Mummy and I made many visits to the Jamaican Embassy for an interview to explain the reasons why I should be able to leave my homeland and move to New York City.

I guess hundreds of Jamaicans had the same idea, because before five in the morning, hundreds of people were already in the line. They too hungered for the American Dream. The lines were extremely long and for months we never made it inside the building to get an interview, but one day we did.

That morning Mummy woke me up at 3am to make sure we got inside the building. Sitting in front of the consulate officer, Mummy was prepared to answer every question.

"Life is difficult."

"Her mother is mentally ill."

"She can have a brighter future."

"I can't afford to take care of her."

The consulate officer was apparently convinced, because six months later the letter of approval came in the mail. My green card was approved and finally my ten-year-old feet would walk down those gold streets.

Everyone in our neighborhood was extremely excited. Our next-door neighbors brought us over huge baskets of mangos, Smith quit cursing at Mummy, and Ms. Cora the landlady invited me over to watch her TV. America was bringing blessings already. That night in Ms. Cora's neatly furnished living room, we sat there with our pinky fingers lifted up sipping on hot cocoa and chomping on hard-dough bread with butter. Mummy requested Marcia, the town's dressmaker, to design the most beautiful white dress with purple stripes for my send off. It was a celebration of my pilgrimage to the land filled with Twinkies, peanut butter sandwiches, and fruit cups.

The night before my flight, it was tradition to have a few people from the block come over to pray and party. For everyone on our street, this was huge. We ate roasted corn with fried snapper, roti, and drank kola champagne. The drunken men entertained us with made-up stories about their adventures and the brutal fights they won back in the day, while the women humored their fantasies and laughed among themselves because they knew most of the stories were not true.

Eventually the festivities fizzled out, and one by one the neighbors straggled home. Whoever was sober enough to pray stayed and prayed until they thought God heard. Mummy and I spent the night packing the rest of my clothes. Her silence let me know she was going to miss me.

"I am sorry, Mummy, that I have to leave you," I told her.

She grabbed my face with both hands. "Don't you ever apologize for your blessings. When good things happen, we celebrate! Make no apologies."

That night while stuffing the rest of my clothes in my suitcase, Mummy pulled her Bible from under her pillow and handed it to me. This was her most valuable possession. She did not have land, money, or any trust fund to pass on but she thought the best thing she could give me was God's word. "When you go to America, I want you to memorize the twenty-seventh Psalm," she said, then recited it with authority.

"The Lord is my light and my salvation, who shall I fear.

The Lord is the strength of my life of whom shall I be afraid.

When the wicked, even my enemies and foes come up against me,

They shall stumble and fall.

Though an army besieges me, my heart will not fear. I shall be confident.

Though my mother and father forsake me, the Lord will receive me."

"Hide this word in your heart," she said firmly. We lay there wide-awake into the wee hours of the morning talking about what was next for us. Our lives were going to change. When one person leaves for the States, they carry not only their dreams, but everyone else's. Even the crickets outside our bedroom window sounded as if they were rejoicing. Before we knew it, it was daybreak. The big day was finally here.

The drive through Port Royal on our way to Michael Manley International Airport felt like a field trip, only this time I was not returning to the home I knew for the past decade. It was time to grow and discover the world I daydreamed about in my corner of the bed against the green wall.

Standing in the line at the airport, a woman in a blue jeans skirt and a colorful shirt stood in front of us. Her dreadlocks were wrapped perfectly around her head in a Rastafarian scarf, and from the back her hair resembled a lion's mane. Everyone who passed by her showed reverence as if a queen was in their presence. It was no other than the beautiful Rita Marley.

When I discovered who she was, I wanted to speak with her, but Mummy was bashful. "She needs her privacy. Leave her alone, Jozanne."

This was my opportunity and I did not want to miss it. Gently, I tapped her on her back. She turned around with a huge and said, "Hi, sweetheart." Her voice sounded like a song. She was a woman, strong and regal. I have never seen such confidence in a woman with that shade of black skin. Her smile was wide and her eyes carried wisdom.

There were no words coming from my mouth, only a huge grin on my face. Rita Marley embraced me with all the love she had inside her. Her hug had no fear. She had seen the world and had a freedom that I had never seen in the women I grew up with.

"Spread your wings," she said as she walked away. It was a sure sign that things were going to be great.

The ticket was in my hand and we stood to the side waiting to meet the flight attendant who was assigned as my chaperone. Mummy took those last moments making sure every hair on my head was in place. Through the crowd I saw Smith with a brown paper bag in his hand and I knew he had not forgotten my beef patties.

A tall, slim, Caucasian woman with yellow hair walked up. No doubt she was from the valley or Laguna Nigel. In her high-pitched tone she said, "I am Becky, your chaperone."

It was time to go and no one wanted to say goodbye. Mummy choked on her tears as we shared one last hug at Gate 45. And for the first time, Smith showed emotion. He handed me my beef patties and hugged me real tight. "Go make something of yourself, Jozanne."

When I stepped onto the plane, from behind the Jamaican citizens pressed their faces against the glass window and waved as all the passengers boarded. From where they stood the future ahead seemed bright and hopeful. It was time for takeoff. Becky buckled my seatbelt and soon we were twenty thousand feet in the air. The clouds were thick like cotton candy. Jamaica was a thousand miles away, and the peace of knowing I would not bump into Jean settled my fears.

Seven hours later we landed at John F. Kennedy Airport. The passengers clapped victoriously. Exiting the airplane, the crisp air cut through my dress as we entered baggage claim. We were in New York City and there were white people everywhere. Everyone seemed as if they had to be somewhere really important.

From a distance my father held high an enormous sign with my name written in bold black marker. JOZANNE. Beside him were my Auntie Rosie, and my two half-brothers, Winston and Richard, who I was meeting for the first time. We got into Dad's beige Chevy van and cruised down the expressway to the boogie down Bronx. The streetlights lit up the highway as if it was Christmas. From the back seat, I peered over Dad's shoulder to see the gold streets, but there were none in sight. It didn't matter. All that mattered was being with my father.

When we arrived at our destination, Auntie Rosie said, "This is your new home, Jozanne." We climbed up a huge set of steps into a courtyard and the brownstone buildings were high to the sky. They were called the Projects.

THIS IS MY NEIGBORHOOD

The Bronx is where I live
Drugs is what they give
Dealers feeling dandy
On the corner selling candy

NO GOLD STREETS

Homies chilling in the cut
Roughnecks too cool to say what's up
Some might think this is no good
Hold on, it's my neighborhood

The Bronx is where I live
Rappers' beats be fluid
Shorties slinging Reeboks
Homies spitting sweet talks
Hip hop, playing bee-bops
Five–O cruising non-stop
Some might think this is no good
Hold on, it's my neighborhood

Compared to the two rooms we lived in on Milk Avenue, the Projects were like Beverly Hills.

"So your grandmother finally got you to come live here," the fair-skinned lady who showed up with Dad when I was six said sarcastically. She was my stepmother.

Dad took me aside to the room I would be sharing with my two brothers and emphasized, "Jozanne, you can have anything you want in this house, just don't touch what belongs to your stepmother. If you see something you like, I will buy it for you."

It was already obvious my stepmother disliked me.

That winter we went shopping for school on downtown 34th Street. I learned the *Star Spangled Banner,* and Shaniqua Jones and I became best friends at P.S 29. Adorned in pink pants with a black leather top and sandals drew me much attention in the hallways the first day of school. Although it was getting a little chilly, I hated wearing those huge Alaskan boots, but after a few frost bites the winter let me know I was no longer in Kingston.

My Jamaican patios slowly blended with the American twang and I learned how to walk with a bop, flip my hair, and throw away the crust of my bread. Nothing beat Kung Fu Saturdays with Bruce Lee, barbecued spare rib tips from the Chinese restaurant at the corner, and playing a game of Double Trouble with my brothers. This became our family routine every weekend. My older brother was the jokester and the younger was the ladies' man.

After school was usually a blast. When we finished our homework, my brothers and I gathered in the living room to watch *Wheel of Fortune* and *The Cosby Show*. Soon my brothers became engaged in football practice after school, allowing me more time with my father after he came from work.

One particular evening while my stepmother worked overtime at the hospital and my brothers stayed back for football practice, my father and I watched a baseball game in the living room. Jose Canseco had hit a home run and Dad was extremely happy. He grabbed me and hugged me tightly.

"I love you," he said.

"I love you too, Daddy."

He squeezed me against himself and I felt everything in his body pressed against mine. My mouth clamped shut and the memory of Roy came rushing back. He lifted me up and embraced me some more. I kept hugging his neck, no words coming out of my mouth. Confused by the expression of his love, all I could do was rest my head on his shoulder. Daddy's love had mixed messages. We were clearly not speaking the same love language, but having a father's love was what I needed, so I never said a word.

What does a ten-year-old child say? Should she scream? Does she tell him to stop? Should she run outside and yell "Help!" as if her house is on fire? No, most of the time children are confused and embarrassed. The love they have for their parent takes over the discomfort they experience.

That's what it boils down to. Love. Children desire to be loved and will accept it any way they can get it, even if it hurts. Child molestation is a play on power and deceit. It's often not aggressive; a subtle touch; manipulation. The violence seems harmless. It controls victims, and controls the people who are blind to its evil.

Most people will scream for help if their house get broken into, but when a person is sexually violated, they usually become silent. Yet when we are violated sexually, our spiritual house is on fire. Someone intruded without permission and has stolen valuable goods, like our confidence, purity, our voice, our self-esteem, and most importantly, our identity. This person is potentially robbing the victim of opportunities for years to come. For instance, the kind of men they will choose, the way they deal with relationships, and how they will show up in the world.

The more frequently those incidents took place, I found it difficult to hold my urine. The World Health Organization states that *"some physical indicators of child abuse are bedwetting and fecal soil way beyond the usual age."* I was ten years old and wetting the bed became a regular thing at night or wetting my pants right before I entered the house from school.

It was October and my brothers began spending more time after school for football practice. One Friday evening after another episode of wetting myself, Dad scolded me, "You need to stop drinking so much liquid. Take a shower and clean yourself up. Jozanne, you are a big girl now. Go smell sweet for Daddy."

His words were smooth as butter and he knew exactly what to say to make me question my judgment. I wanted him to feel proud of me. Whatever he wanted me to do, I did. I entered the bathroom and took that shower. From behind the bathroom curtain, I saw his black work boots through the slit in the curtain. "Dad, don't come in!" I yelled.

BEAUTIFUL

"I am your father," he assured me.

Nervously, I grabbed the towel quickly from the rack.

"Let me dry you off," he said

UNSPOKEN WORD

Shhh. Keep it a secret, he said

He watched me

He washed me

He wiped me

And it hurt

Unspoken words

Wrapped in my emotions

Sitting on the tip of my tongue

Searching for where I belong

Too young to feel this way

What is this game we play?

Shh. Keep it a secret, he said

Unspoken words

"You are beautiful," he kept saying. This kind of beautiful was awkward, uncomfortable, and shameful. I sat there on the bed staring at him, but he never looked at my face.

"I love you," he convinced me. Once again his charm and confidence silenced my inner instinct to scream that I was in danger.

He is bigger. He is right. He has authority. He is in control and you are not. You are just a child.

Children are most prone to feel obligated to please and protect their guardians. In some way they feel responsible that they have brought this ugliness on themselves. My father's unwelcome touch taught me that my body was not my own. I did not have the right to speak up or defend myself. Most of all, at a young age, the word "beautiful" took on a different meaning. Being beautiful meant you were good for one thing: sex.

This was typical male behavior from men I encountered as a child. I grew up witnessing women yielding to the manipulation of sexism in my country. The men did whatever they wanted. Men would grind their private parts on the women at parties, make sexist remarks about their body parts. The women in my vicinity were given no respect when it came to their bodies. Their bodies belonged to the men whenever they wanted it. They were objects. They were helpless. I saw these women in the marketplace. I saw them at church. I saw them on the street walking with their husbands who had found pleasure under another woman's sheet the night before, yet they never said a word. These women cooked, cleaned, and gave to their men whatever they wanted despite the ridicule and shame they received. Here I was at the age of ten, voiceless, afraid, and defenseless, just like the women I grew up seeing. The only difference was this man was my father.

I could not help but blame myself. Maybe I wanted it. Maybe I was too pretty or too sexy. Maybe my rump was too big. Maybe my thighs were too thick. Maybe my lips were too plump. My body had become a curse that made grown men do horrible things. I felt this darkness sweeping over my womanhood, like a thief in the night. The once sacred thing was no longer consecrated. My vagina, my breasts, my shape, everything about being female was unprotected, preyed upon, and taken advantage of.

I was no longer a human being, only fragmented into little body parts and deceived that sex meant love. I was to be the pleasure of any man that wanted a piece of me, and the sad thing was I had no choice to say no. At least that was what I believed. My body did not belong to me. It belonged to a man. He had authority over me. I was made for his pleasure and he had no responsibility to keep me safe and love me.

This was the first lesson about womanhood my father taught me.

This is not God's plan for mankind. A parent's responsibility is to stand guard over their child's soul. It is to train their minds to accept nothing less about themselves than who God says they are. A father is one of God's main tools to teach a girl what she is worth. Parents are God's design to express Himself as a Good God, a righteous father, a protector, and a provider, that loves unconditionally. Parents are God's workmanship to express His heart as a Heavenly Father. It is one of the ways God reveals himself. But when a parent, or specifically a father, abuses his child, it kills faith in a Good God.

An angry Earthly father creates an angry Heavenly God. An abusive Earthly father creates a non-existent, apathetic God who only uses us for His own good. This God is indifferent to our humanity. He doesn't care what happens to us. This God becomes selfish and self-seeking. Who would want to serve that kind of God, right?

When parents abuse their children, they can destroy their faith in a loving God who wants the best for His children. Many will ask, "If God so loved the world, why did He allow this to happen?" God is not a puppet master pulling strings. He is a loving father who does not take away our free will. People choose to do evil things. Because God's heart only abides in love, God has given every man on Earth freedom, the power to choose, to co-labor with him in doing good or refuse his loving ways and do evil. I know parents are human beings and make mistakes, but crossing sexual boundaries is simply an abomination in God's eyes. Whenever a parent violates a child sexually or other abusive ways, it will always result in shame.

Shame disconnects us from intimacy with God. It leaves us feeling worthless and dirty. That is exactly what happened in my life. The very person I loved tainted my view of authentic love, and most importantly God's unconditional love for me. Regardless of how many people told me I was beautiful, I never believed it.

BURN THIS BABY DOWN

What happens when love is awakened too soon?
It flickers and sparks
And soon the darkness barks
Burn this baby down
Burn this baby down
She is young enough
Handcuff her stuff

What happens when love is awakened too soon?
It blazes like a fire
Her shadow becomes the truth
Her true self masks as the liar
Burn this Baby down
Burn this Baby down
She is sweet to keep
Zap her strength and poison her sheets
Just burn this baby down

What happens when love is awakened too soon?
She dies a thousand times
Flat line her heartbeat
Always looking for sign
Watch her strut these streets
Burn this Baby down
Burn this Baby down
She is young and fun
Steal her goods and use her until she is done
Just burn this baby down

BEAUTIFUL

My father ignited shame when he took my hands and crossed me to the other side of womanhood. It was not my time yet to dive into a sea of emotions my soul was not mature enough to carry. The tug of war between my youth and his debauchery became tiresome. His lustful advances told me I was grown at ten years old. Conflicted between allowing him to please himself or expose his deceit, I promised to keep his secret, hoping one day he remembered I was his daughter.

No one knew the secrets behind the perfect father-daughter relationship, except for my stepmother, I assumed. She watched me like a hawk and her unconcerned eyes let me know she cared less if I was around. I tried bonding with her by wearing her perfume from her dresser, and painting my nails with her nail polish, but my closeness only infuriated her jealousy even more. She was also a woman scorned by the betrayal of my father's libido and I couldn't understand why she did not see my signals for help. The closer I got the more she hated me.

However, I don't blame her. She too felt the shame of a flawed husband she didn't know quite well and was too afraid to confront. He was flawed, lost, and obsessed with his daughter's youth and beauty. Both of us were carrying our own burdens too heavy to bear, much less to disclose. Instead, we pretended all was perfect and every now and then we came up for air, we tried to be somewhat cordial with each other.

Soon I found myself often scrutinizing my body in the mirror, wondering what he saw in me that allowed his manhood to trample on his conscience. I barely had breasts and my frail, thin body did not carry any shape like the girls in the magazines my brothers hid under their mattress.

The courage to tell him to stop seemed lofty. The words "No" or "Stop" had too much value, and deep inside I believed I was not worth a penny. Therefore, many afternoons, my father had his way with me when no one was around. My golden streets melted in lava and I was swimming upstream without anyone coming to my rescue. When we don't get the help we need, we drown in our situation. My brothers became envious of my increased allowances and dismissed punishments. Family members passed me daily and didn't realize that my sudden coldness and increased violent temper was the result of my virtue being stolen.

The child who stood up to Miss Miller on Duke Street vanished on Allerton Avenue. She was no longer brave. She had lost her fight. She vanished in his arms. Have you ever felt like your fight wandered off somewhere? The fire you once had disappeared? Too much has happened and your energy is zapped by the disappointment, the fear, and the confusion of abuse. We convince ourselves no one sees our pain. No one understands our circumstances. Like a flower without water, we shrivel up inside and eventually we become invisible.

God is not finished with us yet, although it might not feel like it in the wee hours of the morning when the dark night of the soul challenges our faith. He sees us. For *"the eyes of the Lord are in every place, keeping watch on the evil and the good."* Proverbs 15:3.

When we are in the midst of the storm it is difficult to believe God is Emmanuel (God is with us). Our turbulent life disagrees that God is in control and there is truly light at the end of the dark tunnel. Our boat rocks and the Master is nowhere in sight. Our golden streets are now rocky mountains and we feel cast away. Beautiful, God will never throw a curveball without preparing us for a homerun. We must get up, keep playing the game of life, and believe in our hearts that we can never take a step of faith and not collide into the promise. *"The steps of the righteous is ordered by the Lord."* Psalms 37:23. Yes, even the abused child. It is not over for her. She has a future. *"For I know the plans I have for you, declares the Lord, plans for good and not for evil, to give you a future and a hope."* Jeremiah 29:11.

When our gold streets turn into a dark forest with thorns and weeds, we can call on the name of the Lord in this lonely place. There is no darkness dark enough that God does not see. Even through the darkness *"I run to you, God."* Psalms 31. *"Keep me from the trap that is set before me...For you shall show me the wonders of your love when I am in a city under siege.* " When we are in trouble, *"those who call on the name of the Lord shall be saved."*

God is faithful and we can count on Him in times of trouble. We are never too young or old to cry out to God. He will answer us in the most mysterious and miraculous ways.

The places in our lives that have thorns and thistles don't have to remain a deserted place. God is ready to cut down, uproot, and dig up all that doesn't belong in our lives. We don't have to perish beneath its fury; we can get up, leave all of our old, tattered belongings, and start afresh. We can build our own streets on the truth of God's promises and thrive in our own spiritual houses.

It always fascinates me when I see an old building demolished and a new one arises. That once old dilapidated building is razed to the ground and the thought of a new one is left to our imagination. There is a great architect who already has a vision for the finished product. Soon we see the construction workers laboring tirelessly to bring the vision to life.

The foundation is set, the walls are built, and the roof is on. Inside, everything is designed to fit the needs of those who will live in that house. It gets painted, furnished, and the house has all it needs. People who have seen the old house look in awe at this new building in admiration. We too are like houses. We get banged and bruised up by the climate of our lives. The people around us no longer stare in awe. But one day the great architect, God, sees value and decides to demolish the old you and build a new you.

He has a great plan in place. He begins to lay an even stronger foundation, build us up with his word, and cover us with his love. He furnishes our insides with beautiful things, like joy, peace, and faith. Soon the people we used to be no longer exist. Our peers become witness to the miracle of a new us. Trust me, God has a plan and He can make all things new. The same unfruitful ground on which we once abided can be the very place God gets the glory. He is more than capable of making beautiful gardens out of graveyards.

God is not finish with you yet.

CHAPTER 8

SECRET OUT

Pizza Monday at PS. 29 in the Bronx was every student's favorite. Shaniqua, my best friend, and I left the noisy cafeteria for our hidden spot under the staircase outside. There we boasted about the wonderful things we did over the weekend. Shaniqua's mother had taken her to see a Broadway play and allowed her to have a sleepover with friends. While she boasted about her fun weekend, I wanted to share the incident that took place on Friday evening. It had left me scared, confused, and trapped.

"My father touched me here." I pointed downwards. Ashamed, I looked at Shaniqua's puzzled and distraught face. A part of me wished she'd said, "My dad does that all the time." Instead, her eyes popped opened and she blurted out, "My daddy doesn't do that!" I quickly covered her mouth and made her promise to keep it a secret.

Walking away from the conversation, I feared my secret getting out. I did not want to betray my father's trust. *He will never love me again,* I thought.

It was important that Shaniqua keep my secret. The greatest enemy to freedom from abuse is the secret we conceal. Most victims of molestation are willing to carry it to their graves. They carry the confusion and the burden to protect a family member. All of this leads to one emotion. Silence. No matter how much a child tries to break free, children are children and their need to be trusted and to love others makes them the most vulnerable.

Children fragile hearts are connected to those in charge of them; their desires to connect and reciprocate the love to their parents are just as important. One of the places children learn to commit, show affection, and bond with another is within the family structure. It is innate for children to want to please those in charge of them.

Unfortunately, over 90 percent of sexual abuse is perpetrated by someone a child knows, loves, or trusts. Children are taught to "behave" so they may abide by an abuser's wishes to keep the abuse "just between us." In many cases, children love their abusers…parents, grandparents, cousins, aunts, uncles, close family friends…and don't want to disappoint them. *"In some cases of child sexual abuse, the child victim may actually be 'in love' with the abuser and want to protect that person."* (National Association of Adult Survivors of Child Abuse)

It is important that parents and teachers educate children on safe and unsafe secrets. For example, telling a child that a safe secret is like surprising someone for their birthday or Dad not telling Mommy about her Christmas present. It feels exciting and fun. An unsafe secret leaves you worried, scared, confused, and anxious. No one but you and the predator knows.

This secret, *EVERYONE* should know.

The consequences of holding harmful secrets allow a child to lose their sense of reality. Subconsciously, they create a make-believe world in their mind, pretending to be happy. If not taken care of, this child can become physical ill, delusional, and create personalities that comfort them. There are several behavioral indicators. Children can become clingy, have fits of rage, problems at school, depression, poor self-esteem, fear of the dark, and inappropriate sexual conduct.

After sharing my secret with Shaniqua, I knew there were consequences for my actions if anyone found out. These are some of the reasons little girls and boys keep silent about rape, molestation, or whatever kind of abuse they experience. Child abuse forces children to make grown up decisions. Like, where will I live? Who will take care of me? These are things a child should never have to think about.

The biggest fear of a child who is being molested is being removed from their family. Instantly, they lose their childlike faith in a "Good God" and they find themselves thinking about how to survive on their own. It was vital that Shaniqua kept her promise, so I prayed and prayed every morning to God just like Mummy taught me that Shaniqua kept her mouth shut.

The leaves were shedding and the chill from our bedroom window made it clear that autumn was here. It was the middle of October and Ms. Hamburg, the guidance counselor, knocked on the classroom door one morning while I was in math class. "Can you excuse Jozanne for a moment?" she asked the teacher. I quietly placed my notebook in my bag and exited the class.

"How is everything going, Jozanne?" she inquired as we walked down the hallway.

"Fine."

I was not a simple child. I knew this was not just a regular conversation and I planned on lying my way out of the situation.

We entered her well-decorated office and she handed me a can of Coke. "Have a seat," she said. After each sip, I avoided any form of eye contact.

"Jozanne, how is it living in America?"

"I love it."

"How is everything at home?"

"Good."

After the pleasantries and indirect questions, Ms. Hamburg got straight to the point. "Jozanne, how is your relationship with your father?"

"My daddy loves me."

"How does he show his love for you?" I remained quiet. "Jozanne, do you mind sharing with me what you shared with your friend?"

That day I begged Ms. Hamburg to send me back to class.

"You don't have to be afraid, we will protect you, Jozanne," she assured me.

We sat in her office for what seemed like a lifetime. Seeing the fear on my face, Ms. Hamburg reached in her drawer, took out a yellow writing pad, and placed it on the top of her desk with a pen. "If you don't feel comfortable speaking about it, can you write it down on this notepad?"

I sat there staring at the paper, contemplating whether to write something fictitious or pour out my ink on the truth. The pen in my hand had power to free me from all my secrets and shame, but I was terrified.

"He touched my breast," I scribbled on the writing pad. I was not brave enough to share all the other places he touched. The need to protect him from humiliation became my only concern. There was no way I could write how much I hated my thighs, my lips, and everything else about my body. That little girl running around the yard with a one wheel cart was gone and the thought of losing my father in the process was too weighty for my young heart to handle. My father's affection was like gold and his thoughts of me were like air. He had become my lifeline, and protecting him was my only concern.

Millions of abused children across the world protect the adult instead of speaking out. They decide to be the provider of security, the comforter of broken individuals, and the safety for their perpetrators in exchange for not being abandoned. The truth frightened me. It had too much power to destroy my father, and possibly destroy the people I loved. This is a common emotion of abused children.

Sitting in Ms. Hamburg's office with the truth inside of me felt lonely. It was as if I was the only girl in the world this was happening to. I was not ready to be heard or seen in that way. I did not want to be seen as the little girl who was abused by her father. Daddies were to love their daughters. My daddy was not supposed to be this kind of person. He was different in my mind, and wrapping my mind around my father hurting me in any way was inconceivable. I had painted a perfect image of him from I was a child back in Jamaica, but this was not the man I came to know. He had deeply rooted issues that no one knew about.

I handed Ms. Hamburg the notepad and she read it without any visible emotion. A brief silence stood between us. She knew I had more to share. "Your secret is safe with me, Jozanne," she said. The lump in my throat felt as if it was cutting off air from my lungs. Finally, she gave me permission to leave and I ran down the hallway back to class.

Shaniqua stared from across the room, but I was too inflamed about her slippery tongue. I vowed to never speak with her again. Two people had now become a witness to my shame and with uncontrollable tears I buried my head on the desk. For the first time I missed my corner of the bed against the green wall back in Jamaica.

Before I could blink an eye, Thanksgiving was a few days away. My stepmother, my brothers, and I had just gotten back from Pathmark Supermarket when the doorbell rang. It was a slender African-American woman with a briefcase in her hand.

"Can I help you?" my stepmother asked.

"My name is Mrs. Thompson, and I'm from the Child Welfare Bureau. Is Mr. Henry McPherson available?

My brothers and I were immediately sent to our room. All three of us tried listening through the walls but the conversation was unusually quiet. My brothers questioned me about the woman in our living room and I pretended I had no clue who she was. Suddenly the door slammed shut and I heard my dad's footsteps thumping towards our bedroom. He pushed the door open.

"Jozanne, have you been telling people at school that I am touching you?" My brothers and I sat there stunned. My stepmother glared at me and shook her head in disgust.

"No," I said.

"Jozanne, have I ever touched you inappropriately?"

"*Yes*," I responded under my breath. The room went so quiet you could hear a pin drop. That affirmation was strong, clear, and certain.

The secret was out. My secret was out. My heart was beating fast and father's eyes pierced through my soul.

It was the first time I saw rage and disappointment in his eyes.

"I told you she would bring problems to dis house," my stepmother said.

They pulled me to the living room so the conversation was more private. My father proceeded to ask me again, "Jozanne, have I ever touched you?"

It startled me that he was lying when he told us to always speak the truth. As if this was some sick game, I stood there perplexed.

My stepmother questioned, "Where did your father 'touch you,' Jozanne?" she asked sarcastically.

"Here and there," I told her, pointing to my private parts.

"The only time I did such a thing was because you urinated on yourself and I helped dry you off," my father defended.

I tried explaining how it made me feel, but he walked away before I could. My stepmother followed behind him with a sneer on her face. My *yes* had created enemies. I sat there in the living room questioning myself. Had I imagined all these things in my mind? Maybe I misinterpreted his action. Maybe he accidently pushed his finger "there." Maybe the burning sensation I felt after he was done was because I peed so much on myself I had an infection. Maybe I just did not understand what a father and daughter relationship should be.

Or maybe I was crazy just like my mother.

That night no one spoke. The secret being out will not only silence you, but silence those close to you, especially if it happens within a family. A gloom was set in the atmosphere and from that day on, nothing was the same. My stepmother headed off to work right after and everyone tried to get some sleep. In the following weeks, the news spread like wildfire throughout the family. My *yes* had created gossip, ridicule, ostracism, judgment, and more silence. No one knew what to do with the truth and their only response was fear.

SECRET OUT

Thanksgiving was now here and everyone at the dinner table knew about Mrs. Thompson's visit.

Auntie Rosie said, "What is dis I hear, you lying on your father? I thought you were better than that. I am disappointed in you, Jozanne. Very disappointed."

Her blaming me for speaking the truth only increased my shame. The pointing of the finger and the false accusations kept my face staring at my plate throughout dinner. Soon after, I dismissed myself from dining room to my bedroom. No one understood. No one ran to the rescue. No one saw past his or her own feelings and shame. That is the response when the secret is out. Only the victim gets to be clothed with its stench and suffer its judgment.

My first piece of turkey with stuffing handed through my bedroom door by my older brother told me I had created a prison for myself. I could hear my cousins running through the hallway, laughing and playing with each other. They wanted to come inside the room and play. "Leave her alone," someone told them. "She is trouble." It was the first time I felt anger and rage boiling on the inside. I wanted to pick up the beautiful vase from my dresser and throw it against the wall. I wanted to scream, run out into the hallway and make a scene, but I did not want to be like Jean. I needed to be soft, gentle, and beautiful, the way "girls should be." That's what Mummy said a thousand times. "Princesses don't dash into anywhere."

Compose yourself and handle your emotions like a lady. Beautiful women don't act like they are wild animals. But how can a girl be well-behaved when someone invades her spiritual house without her permission? How can she contain herself when there is no justice? Why should she be silenced when she has been violated?

This secret was a ticking bomb and I sat there on the bed and no words were coming out of my mouth. It all exploded on the inside and I had to deal with its ruin.

The festivities were over and everyone went home. Dad sat alone in the living room watching television. He didn't want to talk. I apologized over and over again for speaking the truth. This was the beginning of all the unnecessary "Sorrys" in my life. Sorry for being myself.

Sorry for protecting myself. Sorry for speaking what's on my mind. Sorry for making my family uncomfortable. Sorry for being brave. Sorry for speaking the truth. I became the girl with lots of sorries.

Those sorries kept my wounds invisible for many years. Living with the pain of disappointing everyone left me uncomfortable in my own skin. For years I fought for peace by being passive simply to not offend anyone, and one day I found myself a people-pleaser. Afraid to be courageous, afraid to speak my mind, afraid to be different. Silence of the truth will always make us captives and turn us into someone other than ourselves.

Many evenings after that incident, when I came home from school, Dad made his position clear. "Stay away from me. I don't want you going to school telling lies on me." His rejection had me apologizing over and over, even when I knew what he did was wrong.

Most people don't become who God created them to be because they are constantly apologizing for being honest, extraordinary, and unique. We become afraid of our own voice, especially when we don't fit in with what the majority feels. I distrusted my feelings, my emotions, and my intuition. Then again, I was only ten years old. Everything I had learned about God at Maranatha Church seemed untrue. Everyone proclaimed the "The Truth will make you free," but this truth persecuted and shamed me. It brought heartache. It left me afraid, unloved, and silenced. In our society, this is the normal response when anyone break their silence. We must stop this.

For five months Dad and I barely spoke, much less stayed in the same space alone, until the beginning of spring break. He entered into my room one evening with my stepmother. "Jozanne, you have brought a lot of problems to this house and we can't keep you here. I have to take you back to your grandmother," he said.

The news hit me like a ton of bricks. This was not the plan. I had made promises to my grandmother that I would make her proud. Be someone. Change the tides of bad luck assigned to us. There was no way I was going back to Jamaica.

Although I kept apologizing, I learned the truth was not worth hearing. The world I lived in preferred fantasy over reality. My friends thought we were the perfect family. There were really no signs to show I was a child being molested. After all, I had good grades; I didn't show any signs of dysfunction; I carried a smile on my face most of the time; I was not reclusive and awkward. I had become a great performer at hiding my pain and shame.

That night as I wept at the edge of the bed, convincing my father I was wrong and promising him I would never say those words again, he granted me no mercy. A ticket was already bought for that same night. I packed my suitcase and we took a one-way flight into the night back to Jamaica.

With headphones plugged into my ears, I pretended to listen to music the entire flight but my heart was shattered into a million pieces. Whitney Houston's *Greatest Love of All (I believe the children are our future, teach them well and let them lead the way)* came on and the tears fell. Confused, I sat 20,000 feet in the sky, powerless, numb, and silent. Why didn't I keep my big mouth shut? Mummy had told me time and time again to keep my business to myself.

The plane landed and we made our way to baggage claim. I lagged behind because I had brought back no gifts. Everyone back home was depending on my success. There was supposed to be a party, but instead it felt like a funeral. I had regretted disclosing my secret.

SECRET

The Secret is a weapon
Masked behind perfection
Shameful in its silence
Powerful when it's spoken

BEAUTIFUL

The Secret is an enemy
Pretends it's a friend
Comfort for the moment
Death to the soul in the end.

The Secret is Truth
Most feared by its oppressors
A teacher of pain
But Freedom to its owner

Secrets of abuse change our lives forever. The fear of someone finding out holds us captive. It keeps us up most nights. The secret becomes more and more burdensome because we become the glue that holds everyone together. The pressure to keep the image of our perfect family, spouse, kids, or community slowly closes in on us, and eventually the people we tried our best to protect become either a stranger or an enemy.

Secrets of abuse come with deep suffering and isolation. No one knew the real Jozanne. I performed daily to be the best for everyone except for myself, believing no one would love me broken. The broken me was not kind, well-behaved, or pure. My secret created darkness inside of me and I wanted no one to see it. But keeping secrets can never heal our wounds and save our family dysfunction. It only deepens the pain and rips everyone apart.

Molestation is shameful for everyone involved, not only for the victim. The perpetrator often experiences his/her own kind of shame. No one wants the light to shine in that nebulous place. While these feelings are real and understandable, God is bigger than our shame. Actually, he came to redeem us from shame. Shame is never our inheritance.

When man sinned in the garden, scripture said, *"They realized they were naked, so they sewed fig leaves together and made coverings for themselves."* Genesis 3:7. But even though they were covered, they still felt ashamed because, *"Then the man and his wife heard the sound of the LORD God as He was walking in the garden in the cool of the day, and they hid from the LORD God among the trees of the garden."* Genesis 3:8. Shame will have us covering ourselves with anything we can find.

Man wanted to keep what he had done a secret from God. Once free, filled with joy and innocence, their eyes were now open to sin and their spiritual position was no longer of authority and confidence. Their shame not only took their identity, but took their position in God. The word "shame" means "to be disappointed, or delayed and confounded."

Does your secret and the shame it carries have you in a place of confusion and overwhelming disappointment? Beloved, there is nothing God can't redeem. God showed us, through Jesus, his plan to help us overcome shame. Jesus is the perfect example of one who endured shame, but what Jesus did was keep His eyes on the victory ahead of Him. He knew that despite the shame He felt, God had a plan for Him. This joy was set before Him and deep in Jesus' heart He knew that without a shadow of a doubt shame was not His identity.

Everyone keeps a secret to avoid shame as much as possible. We fear abandonment and rejection; we worry about losing our dignity and reputation. It's an awful experience and emotion to have. But Jesus despised shame. He was not willing to relinquish His spiritual authority of who He knew God called Him to be just to avoid shame. He knew He had power over shame.

Shame comes to distract us from our purpose and God getting the glory in our lives. Child molestation, rape, and domestic violence are all shameful things for the victim as well as the perpetrator. It reveals sin, it shows imperfection, and in the perpetrator's case discloses the secret things of their hearts. What we fail to realize is that we can find healing and restoration in God. Shame has no power over us, only what we give it.

God has set a plan in place for our deliverance and restoration. While we don't know what that looks like, by us taking a leap of faith to no longer hide behind the secret that holds us captive, God miraculously will give us the confidence and boldness to walk out in the truth about who we are in Him. We will discover ourselves again. Soon shame passes over our lives and one day we will bask in the Son. The secrets we are afraid of sharing are more afraid of us. When we give God our shame, shame can no longer destroy the quality of our lives and keep us isolated. God will not just show us the way out, He will show us the way forward.

"Do not be afraid; you will not be put to shame. Do not fear disgrace; you will not be humiliated. You will forget the shame of your youth ; the LORD Almighty is his name—the Holy One of Israel is your Redeemer; he is called the God of all the Earth." Isaiah 54:4–5. Jesus has taken our shame.

The shame does not belong to you.

CHAPTER 9

WHEN DADDIES GO

THE CAB DRIVER pulled up to Mummy's house in the blackness of the night. She and Smith had moved to another house, renting out another one room to start a new chapter. My knees felt like paper walking up the steps.

Dad banged on the door, calling, "Ms. Dixon, Ms. Dixon!"

The lamplight came on and we could see Smith's silhouette through the stained glass door coming to answer it. "Who is it?" he asked cautiously.

"It's me," I replied. Smith opened the door, looking dumbfounded to see us standing there at one a.m.

Dad handed him my suitcase and pushed his way into the room. Mummy sat up on the bed, looking at us as if this was a dream. "Ms. Dixon, I had to bring her back. She went to school and lied, telling people I touched her inappropriately."

"Henry, I can't afford to take care of her. Smith is the only one working."

"I am sorry, Ms. Dixon, but I don't want her to send me to jail."

"Child, learn to keep your mouth shut," Mummy scolded.

I no longer had a name. I was "she" and "her." No one cared to hear my side of the story. Invisible and silent, I stood there waiting for someone to acknowledge my pain and cover the shame I felt. That is normally how children are treated in this situation, especially in a family setting. Everyone cares how this affects their lives rather than how it will alter the child's perception of the world and their presence in it.

My father handed Mummy one hundred American dollars, kissed me on the forehead, and left once again. I became a pawn on a chessboard, moved by players who wanted to win their own battles. Smith poured himself a glass of red wine. Mummy sat there speechless. The look on my grandmother's face showed how disgruntled she was.

"Put on your pajamas and don't cry," were the only words she had to say. But I couldn't hold the tears any longer. I needed those tears to soothe the scars left on my heart. My father had left with no remorse. I watched from the window as he entered the cab and disappeared into the night. I thought maybe he would find it in his heart to return for me. But he was gone. That night, my father lost his position as a dad in my heart.

When sexual abuse occurs, everyone loses his or her identity. The victim *and* the perpetrator. I crawled over Smith and Mummy back to the green wall and cried me a river. As outspoken as I was as a child, sex was a forbidden topic. We were taught it was grown people's business. Sex and my anatomy were never talked about. I remember once seeing a maxi-pad commercial when I was six years old. The commercial opened with a woman sulking on her couch and after wearing a maxi-pad, she was running through a beautiful green field, free and joyful. When I asked Mummy what was the maxi-pad for, she said it was to help the woman run.

Mummy was a trip, I tell you. No one wanted to talk about the vagina and the penis. That was grown folk talk, and culturally the children in Jamaica needed to stay out of grown folks' business. But despite what Mummy and the rest of parents in Jamaica felt traditionally, us little girls and boys were growing hair on our private parts and experiencing things we were trained to suppress because they were "bad."

In the home where I grew up sex was a bad word. Although I did not have sexual feelings at that age, I was still curious about my body and wanted to know more than what I was being told. It is critical for parents to grant their children permission to express themselves without judgment. A child being able to voice his or her thoughts and concerns on issues, no matter how disturbing or awkward it can be for parents, will prevent years of unnecessary problems in the home.

No one wanted to talk about my body and the sudden pain that came with its assault. For the next three weeks I lost my appetite for the curried chicken, ackee, salt fish, and all the rest of the fine Jamaican cuisine Mummy sat in front of me. My weight had dropped severely and Mummy became worried I was not going to survive.

When fathers disappear, a girl's identity flickers like a candle, and somewhere down the line the light gets blown out. She will have to work twice as hard to find herself in the world. A good father's presence creates the pillar and backbone of a child's growth. Their words become a mandate, setting the path for her journey to herself. I know we live in a society where it has become normal to not have a father in the home, but because we have learned to live without something doesn't mean we never needed it in the first place.

DADDIES PLEASE DON'T GO

Daddy, please don't go
We need to grow
We need heroes
We need cuddles
We need good role models
To fight our battles

When the world tells us we are not beautiful
We need your affirmation
We need your affection

BEAUTIFUL

Daddies please don't go
Daddies please don't go

Hold our hands
When you leave
We bleed
We fight to breathe
When you disappear
We scream for attention in all the wrong faces
We get lost in scary places

Daddies please stay
Daddies please pray
Daddies clean up your mistakes
Daddies stay awake
Anchor our identity in the truth
That God is good.
That God is love.
That God made all things beautiful.

Daddies please don't go.
Daddies please don't go

Between 1960 and 2012, the population of fatherless homes had grown to a whopping sixteen percent increase, according to the US Census Bureau. *"57.6% of Black children, 31.2 percent of Hispanic children, and 20.7% of White children are living in homes absent from their biological fathers,"* says Family Structure and Children's Living

Arrangements 2012. According to the National Center for Fathering, *"72% of the U.S. population is without fathers in the home."*

Fatherlessness is an epidemic around the world. Our society has accepted this as the "new normal." Regardless of the fact that single mothers have held down the household, raised children, and brought home the bacon, nothing can compare to having two emotionally stable and available parents in a home. It brings balance, order, and clarity in a child's life.

My father's constant disappearing act reinforced that commitment and love was scattered and occasional. The acceptance of others not keeping their word became the custom, and holding the "family secret" created more shame. "Don't let the neighbors know what happened," Mummy insisted.

Once again, I found myself protecting my parents. The Jozanne everyone knew in Jamaica became an angry eleven-year-old girl who hated her body and everyone who came across her path. My father had vanished in the middle of the night and I wasn't sure what to do with the love-hate relationship I now had for him.

That spring, Mummy kept saying, "Someday the sun will rise and set in a place you have no choice but to feel the heat." Mummy always had something to say but never came close to addressing the issue of molestation. This topic was still not on the table for discussion. But things were definitely on fire and no one was brave enough to fan the flames. I wanted her to know I hated being a girl. It came with too much trauma. There were too many tragedies around my anatomy. Up until then, no one had told me about child molestation. It felt as if I was the only child who had these issues. The teachers never shared about it in class, no one spoke about molestation in church, and no child ever whispered it to me in secret. Molestation was a weighty word that carried heavy shame and the only remedy was to pretend it did not happen.

Child abuse. We don't know how to deal with it. This kind of sexual manipulation is considered touchy and shameful. When this issue bears its ugly head no one knows how to address it without feeling humiliated. But avoiding it does not make it disappear; it actually becomes the thing that destroys the family unit. Everyone suffers.

Mummy had missed relaying these details on the steps during our evening conversations. She never told me no one was to touch me in that way, or if they did what actions should be taken. She did not tell me that sometimes in disclosing the truth, people prefer to not hear it. She missed out on telling me that when lies are cast on the sea of love, sooner or later the waves will take you under. Mummy never told me about the birds and the bees, or that sometimes bees sting. She never told me that my breasts and vagina were my privacy and it was not up for discussion. She did not share that I lived in a culture of silence when it came to a woman's body and her right to say no was covertly not accepted.

How much should a girl know about her vagina? Why was no one teaching us how to take care of it? Protect it? Know its value? Defend it? Respect it? There was no safety manual for it when it came to predators. Because there were no do's and don'ts, two men crossed their boundaries without any consequence.

Let's talk about sex and the vagina. Growing up many young boys are curious about this intimate part of a girl. To score was the goal most of the time. But no one was teaching men that getting the girl in bed did not make him a man. Fathers normally sit back and applaud when their teenage sons lose their virginity. It was some rite of passage to manhood that made them feel like they conquered. And for the girls, in some weird way, they felt beautiful and valued when the cute guy down the street wanted to lay up with them somewhere. No one was explaining to us girls at the time that our vagina was sacred and the beauty of sex was a celebration and not a goal checked off by a man's ego. Just because a man wanted it and had the desire for some excitement did not mean it was a woman's responsibility to take care of his sexual needs on demand—especially when his action showed no commitment.

The church is also too afraid to address the issues of sex, sex addiction, and sexual abuse. For years pastors preached about sexual purity but shied away from the sexual history of its parishioners. Everyone has a history. People find it shameful to disclose their sexual resume in fear of being shunned by the church, friends, and even potential mates. However, freedom can only be gained through transparency. I am not saying we should go and tell everyone on the mountaintop about our sexual encounters, but at some point our sexual life should be discussed in order for healing to take place.

We live in a society where sex is often paired with shame, especially with females. Our bodies are scrutinized and violated physically and verbally. Women are talked about, laughed at, and visually undressed by men. We endure unwanted comments walking down the street, we spend our moments nipping and tucking to be accepted. Our beauty is oftentimes sexualized.

"Sex sells," they say. But what is the price of sex, really? How many young girls will be sex-trafficked before we realize we are not only having a problem, we are having a love problem? How many children will have their bodies violated before we sit down and have real conversations in our families that there is an issue and we need to address it?

Keep in mind, there is nothing wrong with sex. But sometimes the way we were introduced to sex robs us of what true love and intimacy means. God created us with these anatomies for pleasure, procreation, and the expression of love. But many times sex is driven by lust. No judgment here. Lust's desire is to please itself. It's about the best way we can feel ecstasy, pleasure, have control, and fill our appetite. Lust never comes from a place of deep love and affection for another. The foundation of lust is rooted solely in self-pleasure and if not controlled, it can grow into a monster.

The beast is never satisfied and it will search for pleasure wherever it can be found. Some lustful thoughts, fetishes, can quickly turn into perversion if not addressed. Perversion says, "I need my sexual needs met and it doesn't matter the age. I want you." "You turn me on." "It doesn't matter if it makes you uncomfortable, it makes *me* feel good." As a matter of fact, "It makes me feel powerful and if you don't give it to me, I will take it by force."

These are some of the thoughts in the minds of perpetrators. Lusting after a child doesn't happen overnight. It begins with a thought. That thought lingers and it turns them on. Eventually one day it is acted on.

My father's action left me ashamed about all my woman parts. I hated my breasts peeping through my yellow and white striped shirt in the mirror. My grandmother bought me a training bra, but that only made them look bigger. My breasts were to blame for me being back in Jamaica. Growing into a teenager was unstoppable, and the only way I knew how to handle it was to wear clothes that made me look less feminine.

Everyone was too busy to prepare me for these changes in my body. For the rest of the year, I left my dresses in the suitcase under the bed. I concluded that in order for me to survive, my fists would defend me and a male-looking exterior would protect me from my perpetrators. I became hard, distant, and pensive. Isn't that what happens when we get hurt? Sooner or later the Great Wall of Offense comes up. We come to the conclusion that no one will ever hurt us again. We avoid any contact with vulnerability just to guard our hearts and protect ourselves.

However, we cannot ignore the fact that deep inside we long to be renewed and restored. We miss the softness of our hearts to love unconditionally and the freedom that comes with innocence. We become thirsty, longing for a fresh pouring of His Living Water to cleanse our hearts again. Beautiful, whenever I find my heart drifting into a cold place of resentment and bitterness I run to the throne of grace because I know my Heavenly Father is the only one with the remedy for a heart that is crushed. Sometimes our biological fathers are no longer present in our lives, and we doubt God's love for us. The constant disappointment from the people who are expected to love and protect us creates a false image of an unloving God. Gradually, our hearts become callous and distant.

But we can trust in a flawless God who grants us eternal boldness to stand against those who have stolen love, and desecrated our purity and innocence. God will protect us under the shelter of His wings, he will sing over us songs of deliverance. He will gently whisper, "Come away with me, my beloved, and let me love you." May we give our hearts to the One who is only capable of restoring us and fulfilling our joy. Emmanuel.

Although Mummy made small talk to comfort me, nothing could fix this, not even her Jamaican rum. That summer I roller skated back and forth from the front porch to the gate. The neighbors watched from their houses, wondering why I had returned, but I never made eye contact.

That September Mummy enrolled me in Excelsior Private School and every boy in town had a conversation with my fist. Mummy got real fed up apologizing to all the parents.

"Sharon, I am sorry for Desmond's busted lip."

"Well at least the child is not blind, Leroy. Jozanne is just going through some things right now. I will make it up to you, man."

Turning eleven was difficult. I was bleeding and my breasts felt as if they would not stop growing. For three days I walked around with toilet tissue stuffed into my underwear so Mummy would not worry about losing another child. I literally thought I was going to die. No one told me that this was a normal thing until the bloody sheets gave it away.

"Jozanne, this happens to every little girl," Mummy said.

"*Why*! I don't want to be a girl!" I screamed, stomping around the room. "I want to be a boy. Boys don't bleed, boys don't grow breasts. Boys don't get pregnant and go crazy. Boys are good enough. Boys' fathers don't leave them behind. I want to be a boy. I want to be boy!"

Mummy could not get me in a dress even if she paid me. The rest of the year I wore pants, played dominoes with the elderly men, went to the bar with Smith, and gambled at the machine.

It became crucial to learn how to stand up for myself and survive as a woman. For all I was concerned, when I looked around, men were thriving. Smith, Roy, and my dad had taught me well. They dominated the women they claimed to love. We were weak and always at their mercy. We were their experiment, their punching bags, their maids, their release from a bad day, their secret holders, their puppets, and their leftovers. We were the queens without honor and their lover without commitment. We were their everything and yet they saw us as nothing.

Both chauvinistic men and subservient women gave me the impression that the beauty of womanhood was a curse. Being a woman came with too many problems. Where were our protectors? Where were the good men? They were nowhere to be found and I decided to protect myself. No boy was going to take advantage of me ever again. I was never going to give them the victory of my tears or the privilege of my vulnerability. They were going to gain my respect, and every day after school I made sure I let one of the boys have a good jab in the face.

Too often I hear my male friends ask, "Why are 'these women' so disrespectful, hard, and unloving?" Could it be possible that "these women" have never felt the gentleness and the protection of a man in their home or marriage? Could it be they are frustrated because their men did not rise to the occasion to be present emotionally and physically? Could it be their men abused their trust and took advantage of their love? The bold Eartha Kitts said, "A man always want to lay me down but he is never willing to pick me up."

Women's feelings tend to be dismissed. Our pain becomes weakness, our voice becomes nagging, and our truth becomes rebellion. We are often responsible for picking up the pieces after everything falls apart. We have become the fixer of broken things even when we are broken ourselves. But I pray we will become a generation who will teach our young men to feel proud not that they get laid, but they maintained self-control when love is not present. Let's teach our young men to find honor in how many women they have respected and truly loved and not how many women they got under their sheets. Let's teach our boys that "hitting it" does not make him a man, and "protecting it" is more honorable.

It is important that we stop dismissing these issues by brushing them under the religious and culture carpet. Often, we confuse a woman's assertiveness and boldness for being masculine, but the Spirit of God is not passive or timid. She has every right to stand up for herself when taken advantage of.

When I was a child I thought, well, if I cannot speak, at least let me punch someone. That first semester I fought all the boys at school until Kelton Campbell, the chocolate skinned boy dressed in well pressed khaki shirt and shorts that sat across the classroom from me kept staring. He was the "Brandon Walsh" of Excelsior. Girls giggled and blushed when he entered class. I, on the other hand, stared him down, rolled my eyes, and pretended he was no big deal. Kelton made it his duty to look my direction every day. Soon his attention made me uneasy and every day he was winning on who could stare the longest. After a while there were thousands of butterflies in my stomach. I tried focusing, but every now and then I caught myself peeping over my notebook to see if he saw me.

His gaze reminded me that I had something worth looking at, and soon I found myself making an entrance just like Mummy had taught me. "Princesses don't dash into anywhere, they make an entrance." That day I entered the classroom with a sway in my hips and a more inviting demeanor. Kelton was not looking. His head was buried into his notebook. I glanced over but he made no eye contact. As I took my seat, there was a note on my desk.

BEAUTIFUL

YOU ARE

You are like a sweet pear.

You are like a juicy mango
You are like a Joseph Coat flower
And sometimes you are like yams and dumplings
—Kelton Campbell

The butterflies in my stomach felt like dragons. Kelton and I kept our heads buried in our books for the rest of the class. Outside of my father and Roy, this was the first time a male my age saw me as beautiful and I did not know where to place those emotions.

After school that day I ran home immediately to plan my outfit for the next day. Bursting through the door, I jumped on the bed, yelling, "Mummy, I want to be a girl! I want to be a girl, Mummy!"

"Child, get off this bed. What is wrong wid yu?"

"I want to be a girl! I want to be a girl!"

"Which big headed boy did you meet at school?"

Oh, I could not hide anything from her.

Ransacking through the suitcases left under the bed for months, I searched for the prettiest dress I could find.

Mummy sat there smiling. "Jozanne, I hope it is not that coconut head boy, Kelton Campbell. That boy's head is too big."

Well that big headed boy had me liking my face, my hair, and my voice again. Although this was a breakthrough to some degree, it would the beginning of me being co-dependent on the approval of others. When our only affirmation of beauty and being loved comes from anyone outside of our creator and a loving parent, it leaves us seeking the stamp of approval from those who are just as flawed as ourselves.

Like a drug addict comforts their wounds with narcotics, I satisfied my insecurities with Kelton's adoration and all the men who followed through high school and college. Kelton became the anecdote to healing Daddy's mistake.

A father's disappearance leaves a hole in a child's heart. Fatherlessness creates massive dysfunction in children. It leaves its victim on a constant search to find a place of belonging. The loneliness sometimes draws children to gangs, toxic relationships, and identity issues. My father weaving in and out of my life left me unstable and co-dependent.

In the third chapter of Matthew, we can see God's relationship with Jesus. Jesus had gone over to Jordan to be baptized by John the Baptist. When he got out of the water, scripture said, *"The Spirit of God descended on him like a dove. Then God spoke and said, 'This is my beloved son, with whom I am well pleased."* In that statement we see God's first affirmation was Jesus as His son. He affirmed and validated his existence. Jesus had the assurance of who He was, which gave Him identity.

It was necessary for God to profess his love, but also His acceptance of Jesus as His own son. He affirmed Jesus by ownership. It was this knowing that helped Jesus to follow through with His assignment even though it was tumultuous. Jesus did not need the cross to confirm His identity. He knew who He was while carrying it. He knew who was when He was pierced to it. No trial could make Jesus question his identity. And the only time Jesus cried out in much agony was when he said, "Father, why have you forsaken me?" This demonstrates how devastating the broken relationship between a father and a child can be.

You see, identity is important to our assignment. Rejection and abandonment from our parents, who are in a position to help us discover who we are, make it difficult to fulfill destiny. A child's life becomes a constant battle when those who are appointed to protect and nurture them abuse them.

Throughout scripture, God calls us "sons." Identity comes before assignment. Son-ship is important to God. Relationship takes precedence over everything. God knew a good relationship would bring Jesus into destiny. Purpose and destiny are all connected to the relationships we have from the beginning of childhood and throughout the rest of our lives.

But the question becomes, "What if I don't have a good father in my life? How do I fulfill my calling?" How do we become productive and purposeful in this world, and how do we live healthy lives after a horrible childhood?

I say *FAITH*. Faith is the substance of *"things hoped for and the evidence of things unseen."* Hebrews 11: 1. We set out on the journey to transform our minds to the truth about who we really are. We are not a coincidence; we are not a random thought that exists in time and space. We are designed and thought of with purpose by someone greater than our parents. To some, Jesus was a carpenter. To his Earthly parents he was just a boy. To others he had a gift. But to God He was His one and only Son. He was the Light of the world. A perfect replica of the Almighty God. Jesus had identity. Identity made Him an heir. Identity gave Him access to the kingdom. Identity gave Him the authority He needed to carry out His destiny. Identity re-assured Him He was not alone. It did not matter what others said about Jesus. Identity gave Him the throne.

Simply because our Earthly father abandons us doesn't mean we don't have identity. Too often we define ourselves by our circumstances. For many years, I saw myself as a motherless, fatherless, abused child. These untruths led me to depression and hopelessness. Seeing myself through my experience and background of abuse made life impossible.

However, there came a time in my life where I had to resolve who was I going to be. Was I going to be the abused girl or be who God said I am? After all, He is the ultimate authority. We all were created in His likeness and if we are rejected by our own flesh and blood, it does not mean God is incapable of turning our lives around. God loves to take the most unlikely ordinary situation and make it extraordinary. He said we are fearfully and wonderfully made. We are the apple of His eye. We might not have been created in love by our Earthly fathers, but we were created in God's image. We are precious daughters to the King of Kings.

The most powerful gift God has given any person is *choice*. We can choose who we want to be or who the world and our circumstance dictates to us we should be. All I had to do was believe God's word over my life. Knowing God's love for me and believing it with all my heart enabled me to take my eyes off my circumstances and place it on the truth.

We are loved immensely by God. His love is inconceivable and immeasurable. It is potent. It cleanses. It delivers and it restores us to wholeness. No matter our past, God's love is greater and will perform its work if we let it. Daddies may bail but God's love never fails.

We are never forsaken.

CHAPTER 10

TOUCHED BY GOD

Every now and then when we take a look at the landscape of our lives, we can see the handprint of God. The author and perfector of our faith has been busy writing our story with great plots and twists. Of course we don't feel like God is at work, especially when our trials have turned into tornadoes. Yet if we were to take a panoramic view of our lives we will have no other choice but to testify to the supernatural work of our Creator. God in His infinite wisdom and everlasting love can give us a glimpse of destiny. If we take a microscopic look from when we were children we will see that nothing was by chance. From our personalities to the toys we played with, the things we did, and the people we were drawn to all reveals a part of God's plan for our lives.

It was coming to the end of the semester and the city of Kingston requested Excelsior Private School to present a performance in honor of the Jamaican soldiers at the Wyndham Hotel. Ms. Williams, our art teacher, paced the floor searching for a volunteer. No one stepped forward.

"Jozanne, I am volunteering you for this performance," she said. Had she lost her mind? I could barely raise my hand in class to answer a question much less stand in front of an audience to perform anything. Then she said "Kelton, you and Jozanne will create something for this event." The class roared with laughter, while some of my classmates sang, "Jozanne and Kelton sitting in a tree. K-I-S-S-I-N-G."

I didn't know how I was going to be able to live through this. The butterflies and the puppy love vanished when Kelton came up with the brilliant idea. "Let's sing Dolly Parton's and Kenny Rogers's song *Island in the Stream.*" A song? Are you kidding me? I am not a singer. I can't even speak. *Might as well you take me now, Jesus,* I thought. There was no way I was going on that stage, but Ms. Williams did not take no for an answer. Every day after school, Kelton and I practiced.

This was the first sign from God that He had a plan for my life way greater than how I saw myself. He was not going to allow the shameful things in the secret places have me in hiding. It's just like his character to bypass our fears and insecurities. He takes the incapable and makes them capable.

I am not sure where you are in your life currently, but I can assure you your steps are ordered by God. His penmanship is written in every journey, whispering His love, and any moment he can take our test and turn it into a testimony. Regardless of the trials, God has an amazing plan for our lives that will unfold gradually. *"And the Lord shall guide, He will satisfy your needs in a sun-scorched land and will strengthen your frame. You will be like a well-watered garden, like a spring whose waters never fail."* Isaiah 58:11.

Hardship and tribulations leave us overcast, making the future seem dim, but if we keep pressing forward, surrendering all to our Heavenly father, love and grace will meet us at a crossroads and set our feet on the path of the miraculous.

The day of the performance Mummy dressed me in a light pink chiffon dress, a red hat with a veil, and white gloves. Mummy loved wearing gloves because it reminded her that no matter what we were going through, we were royalty.

"Now remember, Jozanne, princesses do not dash into anywhere, they make an entrance," she said as she placed the veil over my eyes.

"I get it, Mummy. I get it." Still, I was terrified.

"Fear God, not man, Jozanne. They are people like you and me."

Arriving at the Wyndham Hotel was like walking into Buckingham Palace. The doorman greeted and escorted us to our table. I searched the room for Kelton, and spotted him in a nice dark blue suit with a smile on his face, looking like a young Wesley Snipes.

Before we could bat a lash the MC called us to the stage, and from what I can recall the room became one huge blur. Kelton grabbed my hand and pulled me through the crowd in front of three hundred Jamaican soldiers, along with their families and friends. From the stage, the spotlight prevented us from seeing the faces in the audience. I was stiff as a board and Kelton nudged me with his elbow. Some of the soldiers chuckled. One soldier shouted from the audience, "Sing, rude girl!"

The soundtrack began, and Kelton swayed his hips and sang the first note. It was now my turn and with everything in me, I belted out my verse as loud as I could. Jozanne was getting her groove back. That night Kelton and I sang our little hearts out and danced like no one was watching. The audience cheered and laughed at our ridiculousness. We were superstars for four whole minutes.

Mummy was proud as a peacock, telling everyone on her way out of the hotel, "That's *my* granddaughter." Life was feeling glorious once again and the memory of my father and America gradually began to fade away.

The rest of the year Kelton and I spent many days eating mangoes under the Saint Julian mango tree. I discovered that freedom and love are not contingent on a physical location, and resides in our hearts. For a year and half, I enjoyed Kingston and Kelton. The elderly men at the bar became my dads and grandpas, the children in the neighborhood were family, and the shirtless rude boys who sat on our neighbors' walls were my protectors. The one room we lived in wasn't too bad after all. We had love, clothes on our backs, and food to eat. It taught me that no matter where we lived or how much money we had in our bank account, a place where love dwells had enormous wealth.

I loved walking home and seeing the people from the neighborhood sitting at the street corner with wet rags perched on their heads because of the heat. Instead of taking the shorter route home, I took many twist and turns throughout the community. I wanted to discover the world right there in Kingston. Who were these people living in my neighborhood and why did I want move thousands of miles away from them. There was diamonds right where we were if we had taken the time to look for them.

One day as I counted how many steps it took to get home, I bumped into a woman wearing red flip flops. "Jozanne," she said softly. Her voice was familiar and fear gripped my heart. My feet were frozen to the ground, my palms sweaty.

"Jozanne, is that you? It's me, Jean, your mother," she said.

"No, my name is not Jozanne. You have the wrong person."

"Yes, you are my daughter. It's you."

I was so afraid, I could hardly speak. "No, ma'am…you have the wrong person. I am not your daughter."

I took off and ran all the way home. Mummy became frantic; she did not want Jean to find out where we lived. But eventually Jean discovered we were right there in the vicinity.

One evening while I skated back and forth from the steps of the porch to the gate. Jean showed up, rattling the gate and yelling on top of her voice, "MUMMY!"

Mummy rushed out to the porch. "What is it, Jean?" Jean shook the chain off the gate, walked up to the porch, grabbed Mummy by her dress, and threw her head against the wall on the verandah. Blood spewed everywhere. I ran into the house and closed the door behind me. Searching for my shoes under the bed, I felt an asthma attack coming on. I could hear Mummy bawling, "Jean! Jean! Why are you doing this?" I could hardly breathe. Too afraid to face my mother, I ran out the back door to the front of the yard and ran down the street screaming for help.

BEAUTIFUL

Sirens. Police officers. The neighbors watching from across street. It all felt like déjà vu. Once again Jean was sent back to Bellevue Hospital. It wasn't too long before Kelton and my classmates heard the news. History was repeating itself and in the midst of it all God seemed nonexistent. Everything was spiraling out of control, and as if it could not get any worse, Smith lost his job at the airport. Our only option was to move into Smith's sister's vacant house in Saint Ann. This was all the way in the country. I had one more year to finish at Excelsior and Mummy decided it was best for me to stay at a boarding school in Kingston while she and Smith got situated in Saint Ann.

That summer Mummy sent me to live with a fire baptized woman who spoke in tongues named Mother Lewis who lived in Half Way Tree. It was there I learned to read the Bible faithfully every morning, make my bed after I woke up, cook chicken stew, and go to Thursday night tent revivals in the city. Waking up in wee hours in the morning for devotion at twelve years old felt like torture. Mother Lewis literally pulled me out of bed and threw cold water on my face. It was in her home I learned discipline and faithfulness. "You can only go far in life if you are able to endure, be faithful, and master discipline, Jozanne," she would say.

Although I found her quite annoying at the time, I was always prepared Thursdays after school to attend the tent revivals. Hundreds of people travelled from miles in the heat to encounter God. For hours they praised God until they were dripping in sweat. The men clapped their tambourines and banged away their pain on the drums. The women cried and danced away all that kept them in bondage. It seemed everyone was touched by God except me. Some cried, laughed, bowed down, lifted their hands, and some fell out on the floor. They all seemed so free. I wanted that. I wanted God to blow his breath on me. I wanted to dance until I sweated, laugh for no reason, and pray like I knew the answer would come.

One night I decided to take a leap of faith and go down when the pastor issued an altar call. Besides the "Gentle Jesus" prayer, I did not know what to say to God. That night I closed my eyes, clasped my hands real tight, and prayed, "God I need you." It was from the heart. Within a few seconds, it was if someone touched me on the inside and moved me to another place. My body quickened. It was unexplainable. It was supernatural. The tears came gushing down. God had heard me! The one who made the moon and stars I stared at as a little girl had *heard* me.

From that moment I was not the same. God knew me. He saw me. There is nothing like the moment when you come into something bigger than yourself. You know without a shadow of doubt that it is not of this Earth. It is not man-made. It is not ideology. It is supernatural, and it is speaking to you specifically.

How blessed are we to have a God that sees us and is willing to interact with us no matter where we are. That evening, the only thing that held any significance for me was God. Nothing compares to the moment when Our Creator shows His face and speaks a word to our souls. You might say, well, I never had this experience. We all don't have to share the same experience. Just like a father who has multiple children has a different relationship with each, so does God. He knows what we need and expresses himself in ways that speak not just to our minds, but to our hearts.

The human soul longs for an encounter with the One to whom angels bow. This Great King to many of us seems unreachable. We think He will not hear us. We are too young, too old, or too broken. We think we have to come to Him with eloquent speech and have our lives perfectly together. But the God of Heaven says, "*Come to me, all you who are weary and burdened, and I will give you rest. Take my yoke upon you and learn from me, for I am gentle and humble in heart, and you will find rest for your souls.*" Matthew 11:28–29.

When we find ourselves in the dumps, we must remember God will not leave us there. He is a good father who will pick us up and take us to where we belong. He knows how to touch us where no one can, move us, and reveal Himself to us in a unique way that is significant to our immediate need. No one else might understand or have the same encounter because we are all different and God knows what will minister to our individual design. Moses encountered the burning bush; Mary was visited by an angel; John got caught up in the Spirit on Mount Patmos; Peter walked on water; Gideon placed a fleece.

God knows exactly what is needed to get our attention. His touch is not just for experience, but for transformation. We are all built with a purpose, and if we search deeper we will hear small whispers of confirmation of who we are in God. While we are all unique, authenticity and purpose must be sought after. Prayer is one way to activate purpose. A few simple words from the heart will pierce through Heaven's gates and have the Master of our souls come running out. Not because we are perfect, but because *He* is perfect. Love compels Him to attend to our cry. *"Before you call I will answer; while you are still speaking I will hear."* Isaiah 64:25. God is attentive to our cry no matter who we are, what we have done, or what has happened to us. The once conflicted David said, *"In my distress I called to the LORD; I cried to my God for help. From his temple he heard my voice; my cry came before him, into his ears."* Psalms 18:6.

The greatest moments in my life are when I encounter God. Nothing compares to the burning bush experience. It is unforgettable. It is when God intervenes in our consciousness despite the stormy climate of our lives. It is Him saying, *"I am Emmanuel."* God was with me and conveying His love in new ways I had not experienced. I was not home with my physical father but I was getting closer to my spiritual father. The big guy in the sky spoke and I felt a bit safer in a world that had become so complex. The assurance of my Father in Heaven calmed my fears on Earth. Jamaica was starting to feel like home again.

Although out Earthly father's touch might have brought us pain, God's touch restores our joy. God shows us the evidence of his love by fulfilling his promises. He is the father that never leaves us or forsakes us. He is dependable, trustworthy, and faithful. May we always remember that no matter who abandons us, our Creator will never forsake us.

You are seen, heard and loved.

CHAPTER 11

BYE SAINT ANN

THE YEAR AT Mother Lewis's house came to an end and I was back to living with Mummy and Smith in Gibraltar, Saint Ann. Driving up the dusty white hill, surrounded by greenery, cows grazing, small shops, and houses miles apart from each other, I knew this was no place for a city girl.

We arrived at an orange Spanish style house sitting at the bottom of a mountain, and a scrawny white Labrador retriever named Bobby greeted us at the gate. Mummy and I struggled with the suitcases into the house. Smith pointed me to my own room. No more squeezing together on the bed. I was now twelve years old and needed my privacy.

That night Mummy and I sat on the porch as usual, but things had changed so much. Our evening conversations had come to an end. There was absolutely no need speaking if we could not speak the truth. Life in the country was uneventful. There were no kids close by to play with, so Bobby and I chased each other through the yard.

Since money was tight, Smith decided to breed pigs and sell them in the market. Our first pig was a mean sow named Betsy, and my day's chore was to make sure this crazy pig had three meals a day. Soon we had goats, chickens, and another dog, called Prince. Needless to say, each day was quite eventful with all the animals. The only bonding time with Mummy was our long walks into the square on Saturday afternoon to buy groceries for the week.

One Saturday on our way back from the market, Mummy stopped in the middle of the road with a heavy sigh. "Jozanne, I can't afford to take care of you. America is where you belong." I didn't understand what she was saying.

"I want you to call your father and stepmother and apologize for what you did." I stood there stunned, wondering if Mummy had lost her mind.

"I am not calling them."

"Look, child, you want to be like your mother? You want to be here with no future?"

"I am not calling them!" I shrieked.

Mummy stood there surprised. It was the first time I had raised my voice to my grandmother.

"Tell them you made a mistake and you won't do it again. Jozanne, God wants a better life for you. Jamaica is not it, do you understand?" she pleaded.

The woman who once told me I was capable of doing anything was now telling me I had no options. I needed to compromise my convictions and dignity in exchange for a dream. Her words were final as she hiked on up the hill. Panting, I lingered behind, wondering what went wrong with us. She was supposed to stand up and defend me like she did at Saint Georges Girls' School.

But God was going to teach me that in this life we all have to learn how to stand up for ourselves.

When we reached the gate we were greeted by a squealing pig in heat. Betsy busted out of her pen and was chasing Smith through the yard. Mummy and I dropped the groceries and ran inside the house.

"Lock the door, Jozanne. I don't want this crazy pig in the house!" Mummy screamed.

Smith ran through the gate and down the street with Betsy chasing behind him and Mummy shouting from the bedroom window, "Get him, Betsy! He is a wicked man. No good. He is no good, Betsy!" We laughed until our stomachs ached. Eventually some of the farmers in town helped Smith capture Betsy, took her to a boar, and she was relieved.

Later that evening, just like the good old days we sat on the verandah sipping on cups of peppermint tea. Laughter was much needed by all the tension we had earlier. I got behind Mummy with a small toothed comb to make some Bantu knots in her hair. It was the first time in a long time we had bonded. She wanted to know how the kids were treating me in school and also scolded me about the boys, who only wanted one thing.

It was dusk when Smith entered through the gate, drunk as a skunk. He staggered towards the verandah. "Dixon? Dixon, where are you woman? Is the soup ready?" We did not move. Swaying, Smith shambled through the house knocking over stuff. "What have you been doing all day? You good for nothing woman." Mummy had made up in her mind that night she was not going to let him disturb her peace. I quickly followed behind Smith to make him a bowl of soup so he could eat and go to bed without a fight.

Smith entered the kitchen where the huge pot of beef soup sat on the stove. With his index finger, he took a taste, and spat in the soup. "This is what you call cooking?" he mocked.

He took the huge pot of beef soup from the stove and threw it into the yard. It was the only food we had to eat and Mummy had slaved all day and evening to prepare that meal. She approached him. With the back of his hand, Smith slapped her across her jawbone. It was the first time I saw a man literally put his hands on a woman with such violence. It enraged me to see my grandmother handled in that way when she had sacrificed so much for him.

I ran up to him. "Don't you hit my grandmother again! Don't you ever put your hands on her again!" I stood in front of Smith, pointing my fingers in his face.

Smith was not intimidated one bit. He leaned down towards my face, his breath reeking of liquor, "Who are you? Look at you. Nobody wants you. Your own father doesn't want you. Nobody wants you. You just like your mother," he taunted.

While I stood there with my fist clenched to sock him in the jaw, Mummy intervened. "Leave him alone. He is not worth it."

That night in my bedroom Mummy and I sat at the edge of the bed looking at each other for the longest time. Her hair was turning white, her eyes extremely sad, and the wrinkles on her face were out too early. She had stopped dancing. Mummy had lost her zeal, her fire, and definitely her trust in God. I placed a Band-Aid over her bruised knee and told her, "I will call Dad and my stepmother, Mummy. I will apologize."

Life had gotten the best of us. Mummy's spunk was gone and I blamed myself for her failures. She wanted the best for me and I wanted her to be happy. From that day we made many phone calls and pleaded with my family to give me another chance back in the States. The flight was booked, and this time no one in town knew I was going back to America. There was no big sendoff, nor was there any huge welcome once back to America.

Mummy's last words were, "No matter what happens, do not come back to Jamaica."

My father met me at the airport. He made sure to lay down all the rules before we reached the door. "Be on your best behavior. No one wanted you back. I fought for you. Don't disappoint me, and stay away from your stepmother's stuff."

When I stepped back into the apartment, my brothers hardly spoke and my stepmother stayed in her room until it was time for her to go to work. Their cold shoulders told me I was not welcomed. When it was time for bed, my father gave my siblings a hug, though not me. I stood there waiting for his acknowledgement but he dismissed me to my room with a look in his eyes letting me know he wanted another kind of hug.

I tried staying awake that night because I knew he would come. It did not matter that I shared the same room with my brothers. As unbelievable as it sounds, know that the best thieves are normally the ones who can pickpocket you while talking to you. The reason most people miss it is because they are unguarded. No one expects someone to be that bold, and that is how some pedophiles get away with molesting children. It's subtle and unbelievable.

Slightly awake, yet half way asleep, I felt the tugging of my bed sheet. In the dark, he stood at the edge of my twin bed. I did not move. I waited to see if he would leave, but he tugged harder. When there was no response, he took me by the hand and led me to his bedroom. I said nothing. There is no scream for help when the one who is taking advantage of you is the one you need the help from. I became my counselor and accuser all at once.

It took me off the witness stand of my life. I did not have to explain to my family, church, or school. This time I was going to keep my mouth shut. Breaking the silence would leave me exposed and vulnerable to those who were not ready to hear the facts. Breaking the silence came with a great cost. To some I would be the girl who destroyed her family. To others I would become their hero. Some would lift the banner of victory while others wanted to push me into a grave. Breaking the silence definitely came with a cost and a cross, and anyone who dared to speak had better be willing to be pierced to it.

From that night on, whenever my stepmother went to work and my brothers were fast asleep, it was my duty, according to my father, to make it right. It was my fault why his affection for me could only be shown in secret.

I WAITED FOR HIS HUG

I waited around for his hug.
I waited for his love
I waited until the lights went down
And the night came out
He kissed my tears away
I laid there silent
More silent than the night's wind

Being molested became normal. I learned how to mask my shame behind smiles, made up stories about being the perfect family to friends, and soon enough I pretended it did not exist. We went on many family trips, my stepmother became more cordial, and soon I was welcomed at the Thanksgiving table again. Brothers, cousins, aunts, and uncles, they all loved me in the lie. Auntie Rosie was proud to have me as a niece again. I became a master of pretense and no one could tell I was a broken girl.

I WAITED FOR HIS HUG

I waited around for his hug.
I waited for his love
I waited until the lights went down
And the night came out
He kissed my tears away
I laid there silent
Silent than the night's wind
My words suffocated
Behind his control
That he was the only one who loved me
I waited for his hug

The longer the silence, the harder it becomes to break. Months went by, and soon two years had passed. I was now fourteen years old. I thought for sure he soon would stop. But he never came to the point of embracing me as his daughter. His eyes glistened with lust and his wink told me he was too far gone to ever come back to a place where he could truly see me as his child. For two years I hid our little secret in my heart. But was it a secret, or was it that everyone else was denying it? How can everyone in a household be so oblivious?

BEAUTIFUL

I was a daughter in the day and a mistress by night. He eased his guilt with giving me an extra twenty dollars for my allowance and for my fourteenth birthday, a 24-karat gold chain. As if I was a prostitute branded by her pimp, the humiliation became cancerous, eating away at my soul daily. Like with any disease, I searched rigorously for a cure and I discovered mine one afternoon when I met a twenty-one-year-old boy, Marc, who drove the red Acura on Auntie Rosie's block.

Marc was going to fix things. Between speeding 120 mph in his Acura on the freeway with the wind beating my face and the multiple stops at every fast food joint, it took my mind away from home. Still, my sadness was becoming more apparent, leaving Marc concerned every time he dropped me off.

For four months Dad had no clue that I was sneaking off to New Rochelle with a guy six years older than me until one evening when his car pulled up beside Marc's. We had just left the movie theater and our usual routine was to leave me a block away and I would walk home. My father walked up to the driver's window. Mark rolled the window down.

"Jozanne, get out of the car!" my father commanded. I did not move. Infuriated, he kicked a dent into the side of Marc's Acura, and Marc sped off.

From the side view mirror, I saw my father standing in the middle of the street. I knew for sure he was going to kill me. Marc saw the panic on my face. "What's up with your dad? He is acting like a jealous boyfriend."

Although I did not respond to his comment, it dawned on me; I did not have a father.

Once home I locked myself in the bathroom to prepare for his whipping. I could hear keys turning in the front door and the bathroom door came crashing down. He hauled me into my bedroom and every lash across my back felt well-deserved. I was tired of pretending. I wanted him to hit me long enough to hate him, so the truth would come out. A sprained finger, a swollen leg, and the black and blue marks on my body definitely did it.

The sexual abuse was less frequent but still present. I fought daily with rebellion and he charmed his way back into my space with gifts, apologies, and reminding me that he was the only person that loved me here in America. Eighteen years old was four years away and I could not wait to run away from that house. Some nights I prayed quietly to the God who answered me at the tent revival but to me, he was everywhere except in that house.

GOOD OLE STRANGER

Oh, God, where are you?
Come knock on my door, like a good ole neighbor
Why are you always busy saving the world?
When I need salvation
Remember this little girl

Oh, God where are you?
Stop for the poor, like a good ole stranger
Share with me the good news
They say you are coming
But you are not coming too soon

Oh, God where are you?
Come quickly, Speak to me
Remind me that you are good
Carry me home like a good ole stranger
Oh, God I need you.

BEAUTIFUL

Compromise and silence will always take us further in bondage. My grandmother's desire for me to have a better life clouded her judgment. A parent should never hand their child over to anyone they know is abusive. This happens often in third world countries where single mothers living in poverty believe they have no option but to send their children off with these upper class mavericks who promise them a few dollars and a dream.

My dream came with a price and it was time to pay up. In my father's house there were no mansions, only prisons made up of deceit, betrayal, and seduction.

Things are not always what they seem.

CHAPTER 12

A CHILD LOST

I ALWAYS PICTURED the day I became a mother to be an exciting one. I would scream, run around the house, call all my friends and tell them the fabulous news. The man I gave a child to would be the first to know me intimately and we would have many babies to show the world how much we loved each other. By fourteen years old life had not granted me that wish. I was no longer a virgin and being pregnant was the last thing I wanted.

Mummy told me I was born for God's glory, but there was nothing glorious that afternoon when I discovered my period was one week late. Every morning before school I checked for the light red stain on my underwear but after a month there was no hint of blood. My father bought a pregnancy test, and one day after school I sat on the toilet seat and watched the pink line slowly appear on the stick and it dawned on me for the first time; my father took my first kiss, my virginity, and now would give me my first child. There was no doubt he was the father because Marc and I never had sex.

"Get rid of it," he said, as if this was a pimple on my face or some old shoes I had worn out.

We drove down interstate 278 to a private clinic in Brooklyn. A massive amount of people stood in the picket line out front. An angry woman waved her sign in front of my face, screaming, "STOP MURDERING BABIES!" When I entered the clinic, I couldn't help seeing the sad and awkward stares from the teenage girls who were waiting to get rid of their unwanted child, making me question the decision. No one looked happy. The receptionist led us to a counselor's office.

While we waited for her arrival, my father coerced, "Tell them it's a boy from school."

The counselor entered with a clipboard in her hand and questioned me about my pregnancy. I repeated everything we rehearsed. "You can have this baby if you want," the counselor encouraged.

"She wants to have an abortion," my father stated.

The counselor looked to me for confirmation. "Yes, I want to have an abortion," I told her.

Once back in the lobby I watched each teenage girl enter through the sliding doors for the procedure to be done. One girl in a pink sweater held her mother's arm as if she was ten years old. The fright on her face and the tears in her eyes made me wonder who the father of her child was. Despite the situations that brought us there, we had life on the inside of us and we would never have the opportunity to welcome it in the world.

"Jozanne." A nurse took me by the hand and helped me on the bed. She spread my legs and strapped each ankle tightly to the bed. The nurses chatted among themselves about all sorts of things, like what they had for lunch, and where they were going after work. This was just a regular day at work for them. That day changed my life forever.

The doctor hurried in as if he was behind schedule. "Jozanne, it will be over before you know it," the doctor politely explained as if he had done this a million times. "I will count to twenty-two. Just listen to my voice. One, two, three, four, five..." The anesthesia put me to sleep.

I am not sure how long the procedure was but it felt as if I had just closed my eyes when I woke up. The white light above my head made my eyes hurt. I lay there staring into the light for a moment. It was over. My baby was gone.

"Are you okay to walk?" the nurse asked.

A CHILD LOST

"Your dad is waiting in the lobby for you," another nurse added.

I slowly got down from the bed and went to the restroom to change into my clothes. There was no sign of the procedure. It was all cleaned up except for the blood running down my legs. The nurses handed me some sanitary napkins to stop the bleeding. One of them handed me a pamphlet for further instructions in case there was any complications. Although they didn't know, things were already complicated.

On the way home my father stopped by a diner to let the anesthesia wear off completely. We hardly spoke a word or made eye contact. "Do you like chicken fingers?" he asked as he scanned the menu. The waitress walked over for our order. "Give her the chicken fingers and a coke," he said.

The cramps hitting my uterus reminded me that someone once lived inside of me, yet the only thing I could think of was how to be brave for him. He kept his head in his plate to avoid showing any emotions and once again, I pretended to be fine.

Returning home, I envied the immaculateness of the little girls playing in the courtyard. My perception of the world was different from what I dreamt as a child in Jamaica. It was laborious and difficult. For the first time, I wanted to die. I did not know how or when but I desired it. I had tried to fix everyone and keep our family together but I was crumbling.

Isn't it true that we gamble with our lives? We become addicted to fixing others when they are great at breaking our hearts. We believe we can pull out their potential to love us unconditionally. Somehow we wish the person that breaks us open will eventually turn into great, moral, upright beings. We spend years trying to teach them how we want to be treated. We convince ourselves that long-suffering will reward us with value when God's best option for us is to let them go. I had convinced myself that my father loved me. I had fought for him more than I had the courage to fight for myself. Love becomes a dangerous war when it's placed in the hands of those who have no intention of protecting it.

This is one of the reasons women stay in abusive relationships. We long for our abusers to be different. We end up living vicariously through the characters we create in our own heads. It helps us to cope. Most times, they never change. My biological father's love carried thorns and it didn't matter that my life was bleeding; I was willing to hold on just a little longer.

However, it was too late. I had completely fallen apart and my only alternative was Marc. He became my lifeline. The sneaking around had stopped and I stopped caring about what anyone thought. My time with Marc turned into the wee hours in the morning and my dad had enough. After arriving home one night at midnight, my brothers informed me that dad was out driving through the streets looking for me.

That night when he got home he kept beating me until the plastic hanger broke on my hip. Determined to let me know he was in control, he removed his belt and beat some more. I had made up in my mind to not let him see me cry and held my tears until he left the room.

The next morning he told me to stay home so no questions would be asked at school.

"Look what you made me do to you," he said.

Locked in the bathroom, I ransacked the medicine cabinet. A bottle of Tylenol sat there and I yearned to feel what it was like to drift away. I poured all the pills in my hand.

CONFLICTED

Her name was conflicted
Fighting for her rights not to be violated
Speaking truth and no freedom bell rings
To give up a lie only to be rejected

A CHILD LOST

She is left locking horns with the enemy
Always enticing her with a friendly captivity
Change my name
Change my name
She no longer wants to be conflicted

Her name is conflicted
Always trading places for love
Their faces never gave her any hugs
Half-grown with half-sweet fruit
Adam biting into apples
Leaving no juice
The rind of her youth
Too scared to scream
She is conflicted
Stuck between a princess and a queen
Her name is Conflicted

There are times in our lives when we become conflicted between life and death. We believe it's better to throw in the towel. God is finished with us. We are washed up, used up, and forgotten. Yet nothing is further from the truth. Jesus said, *"The thief comes only to steal, kill, and destroy; I came that they may have life, and have it abundantly."* John 10:10.

When life seems unbearable our first thought is usually to check out emotionally or physically. I believe it is in the darkness when God is the closest to us. No, He did not promise us a trial free life, but He promised us a way to overcome through the cross. We will either overcome the affliction or He gives us the strength to go through it. *"Yea thou I walk through the valley of death, I shall fear no evil for He is with me."* Psalms 23:4. We must remember we are never alone in the midnight hour.

Sometimes we become engulfed in hopelessness for such a long time that we believe the only option left is to take our lives. But Christ died so we don't have to face it. I know you might be saying, "People die every day." It is not as we know death. We keep forgetting that we are not our bodies. Flesh goes back to the ashes; a soul falls into the hands of God. Our bodies are merely jars of clay to house our souls for a purpose. I guarantee you that the enemy of our souls prefers if we exit before our time, knowing this way we will not accomplish the purpose of God for our lives!

"'For I know the plans I have for you,' declares the LORD, 'plans to prosper you and not to harm you, plans to give you hope and a future.'" Jeremiah 29:11. Before we came into being, God had a good plan for our precious lives. Many will ask why we encounter these misfortunes. The answer is sin. We are all given a choice on how we shall live, and like I said earlier, some of us chose to sin against our brothers and sisters, not knowing that every sin committed against us tampers with the makeup of our original design.

Just as there is a remedy for all sicknesses, Christ is the remedy for sin. He is well capable of transforming us. If our hearts are still beating, there is purpose for our existence. God has a plan for you and me. To live we *must* live on purpose! The temptation to give in to death is the easy way out. We must stay the course and seek out people who can help us along the way to be strong and courageous in spite of the situation.

The baby was gone and I wanted to die as well. The mental warfare and the road back to healing seemed like a marathon. For those who have experienced abortion, life can be dismal to say the least. We hold onto the anger and disappointment. As result, everyone around us suffers.

I remember one day I was so upset with my younger brother I grabbed a metal candy dish and slammed it into his leg.

A CHILD LOST

As I continued to deny and repress the abuse, other unhealthy behaviors manifested. Unlike other victims of abuse, I did not self-medicate with drugs or alcohol, nor was I cutting myself. My addiction was unhealthy relationships, rage, and frozen emotions.

It took me fifteen years after my abortion to truly express how that situation made me feel. Sometimes traumatic events keep us stuck. We find ourselves mired in clay with no help, and it will literally take a miracle to get us out. King David knew exactly what that felt like in Psalms 40. There David testified, *"I waited patiently for the Lord; he turned to me and heard my cry. He brought me up also out of a horrible pit, out of the mud and mire."* David didn't just stop there; he continued by letting us know that after he waited on God in such a dire situation, God also, *"...set my feet on a rock and gave me a firm place to stand. He put a new song in my mouth."* Those pits we find ourselves are never until death. Once God deliver us, we come out on top. We become stronger. Even our speech changes. *"A hymn of praise to our God."*

Deep within my soul, I blamed myself for never standing up to him. I was angry with the people who never stood up for me. Angry for feeling afraid; angry with my body; angry with my silence; and angry with God. Shame had a grip on me and all I saw ahead was failure. Regardless how people see us, or even sometimes how we see ourselves, the most validated opinion is how God sees us.

God doesn't see us the way we see ourselves. I only saw an unclean, abused girl, but God saw me as beautiful, chosen, and set apart for a higher purpose. God does not see us through time and space. He sees us from eternity. God desires to bring peace, healing, and forgiveness to our lives, if we allow him. Despite the depth of the sin, shame, or the situation we find ourselves in, if we bring any of our problems to God, He will *"be merciful to our unrighteousness, our sins and our iniquities, He will remember them no more."* Hebrews 8:12.

Abortion is a very controversial topic both in and out of the church. Pro-life believers will say abortion is the murdering of a child in the womb. Pro-choice believers question who determines the beginning of life and who should dictate to a woman what she does with her own body. Listen, we can argue this until Jesus comes, but one thing I can say, no matter your belief, miscarriages and abortions are devastating. We cannot deny there was the beginning of life there.

Everything God created, He began with a seed before it became anything. The future of all creation is hidden in creation. Flight is trapped in birds and swim is trapped in fish. Trees are trapped in seeds. A cow is trapped into a calf. Everything God created, He put in it what it should become. In other words, the future of a seed is not outside the seed, it is *in* the seed, and so it is with you. Whatever God places in you—a dream, an idea, a sperm—there is a future for it. But I am not here to debate or judge this issue. I am here to talk about the fact that whether we believe in abortion or not, it emotionally affects anyone who has had that experience.

In 2011, 1.16 million abortions were performed in America, which means one out of three women had an abortion. Although there are many reasons why, I am not here to discuss those issues. It's the aftermath of abortion that we tend to avoid discussing. As a woman it is in my nature to protect my womb. Abortion is a violent act that scars deeply. It is a silent wound that stays with us even after the physical scar has healed. We cannot ignore post-abortion emotions, like guilt, grief, depression, anger, a sense of loneliness, loss of self-confidence, relationship issues, negative views about having children, eating disorders, and anxiety. The list goes on and on.

We don't need to take forever to find healing, however. Healing is available through prayer, therapeutic methods, identifying our losses, and being vocal about our pain. Because of the grace of God, healing is accessible. The grace of God makes us whole. No, it doesn't happen overnight, but it *will* happen.

In Psalms 147:3 Scripture tells us, *"He heals the brokenhearted and binds up their wounds."* We live in a culture where women are ignored and often discriminated against. We are judged more harshly, scrutinized more thoroughly, and often ignored. God is not sexist. When Jesus walked this Earth, He made it a point to extend his grace to women who were considered outcast, underrepresented, and were harshly judged. For instance, He transformed the life of the woman at the well; He showed Mary Magdalene mercy; He made Deborah a warrior.

And he showed Jozanne Marie such astounding love.

We all have suffered loss. It could be a parent, a sibling, a spouse, or even a limb. Despite your loss, God redeems and restores. He can and will use it for our good if we believe. Over the years as I sought my own healing, God has granted me peace regarding my abortion. I no longer blame myself, or judge myself. The future is bright and promising. Healing and restoration takes our participation and God's manifestation.

We must pursue our healing.

CHAPTER 13

RUNAWAY

THERE ARE MOMENTS in our lives when we have to get up, pack all we have, and run to a place of refuge. Running away from toxic environments is sometimes the safest decision we can make to heal ourselves. The only problem is we run from location, but never from the damage done to us.

I was sixteen years old, living in a burning house, and was forbid to leave. The tension in our house was thick; you could cut it with a knife. Not understanding my plight, my brothers became resentful and angry with me for making their home a living hell. The constant quarrels and physical fights between me and my father had taken their toll on everyone. As we grew older, our relationship became quite distant. Spending time away from home brought much relief. The only way to get away was lying about excessive assignments and book reports I had to finish at the library. However, my father was no fool. He eventually caught on and every time I tried to leave the house, he picked a fight.

One evening on my way out I slammed the door behind me out of annoyance. He followed me into the lobby shouting, "Get inside. I am the one paying the bills in this house." Some of my schoolmates watched from the staircase. He yanked me by the collar, ripping my shirt and leaving my breast exposed for everyone in the apartment complex to see. The boys giggled.

While I twisted and turned to escape his grip, he managed to pull me into the house. His punch to my temple made my eardrums pound and my impulse to defend myself earned him the same to his face. I was tired of the hypocrisy, the lies, the manipulation, the betrayal, and now the beatings. Blow for blow, we fought like two grown men. I had lost control, every pent up emotion unleashed in punches, scratches, and bites. My anger was uncontained and my voice was begging to be free.

He grabbed a piece of rubber hose from his toolbox in the closet. "I will kill you," he threatened. I ran to the kitchen and grabbed a butcher knife. Things had escalated. I was standing in the kitchen with a butcher knife clenched in my hand. The man I loved from that small room at 29 Milk Avenue had become my enemy, and for the first time, I wanted to kill him.

He stepped forward with the rubber hose in his hand. "Don't come any closer or I will kill you!" I shouted. Those words frightened and comforted me at the same time. Someone needed to pay for the injustice and shame. Removing his existence seemed valid. The thought of him gone gave me satisfaction. Maybe if he was gone I would not feel worthless. Everything inside of me told me he needed to pay for the pain he had caused all my life. The knife in my hand begged for revenge and I craved it.

I glanced over and couldn't help but see the fear in my older brother's eyes. "Put the knife down," he begged. Fear was never an emotion I witnessed from him. This was his father too. Torn between taking the only father my brothers had and taking vengeance into my own hands, I stood there, waiting for redemption. Someone to speak up for me. Someone to rescue me. Someone to help me make sense out of life. There was no one. Unfortunately, that is the reality of many abused victims when molestation or rape happens in the family. Everyone in the family wants to save themselves from the shame and the only thing they can think of is to blame the victim or distance themselves from them.

That knife in my hand begged for blood; for the blood he took when he took my virginity. I wanted justice. I wanted peace. I wanted to be heard. For the first time, my father was speechless. The choice between murder and suicide competed for my attention. Unsure which would alleviate the agony I felt, I just stood there waiting.

Waiting for an apology. Waiting for his arms to wrap around me, I clenched my redemption real tight. The longer I looked into his eyes, the more I realize we looked alike. This twisted, perverted love and the guilt behind getting used to it. Maybe I *was* the one to blame. I did not scream. I kept it a secret. My voice yearned to be free. To speak every word I had inside of me. Yet all I could do in that moment was scream. I screamed, and screamed, and screamed. I could not stop. The shame was skin deep. It was too difficult to say *you molested me; you never loved me.* Those words were locked into my flesh like a prisoner.

I felt my hands trembling and it dawned on me that I had become just like my mother, Jean. I had lost my mind, was untamed, irrational, and violent. I was now dashing into rooms breaking things and breaking people. I was also a caged girl behind bars, only the bars were inside of me. There was no coming back from this. I had lost adoration, but also honor for the man I was created to respect and love.

I was a different person, not the one God created me to be. The little girl in frilly dresses and gloves was now stomping around in Timberlands and crouching under hoodies. Yes, I was surely my mother's daughter, dashing into everything and everywhere.

The fright on my father's face told me the lines were irrevocably crossed and there was no coming back from it. He walked away; I stayed, clutching that knife. Freedom was seeping through the stuffy rooms full of secrets we lived in, and although I felt courageous, it broke my heart to disrespect my father.

It was time to leave. The misery displayed on my brothers' faces made it plain that I had worn out my welcome. Not sure where to run, I sat there at the foot of my bed waiting. I was not sure what I was waiting for. I sat there for a moment in stillness. I waited some more until God showed up. The scripture my grandmother gave me the first time I came to the United States broke through the window of my soul and shined in the darkness. Psalms 27. *"The Lord is my Light and salvation, whom shall I fear."* This time, it was not just a verse I memorized. It spoke to me. It showed me my reflection. It showed me the truth. It had life. It had power to rescue me. While I curled up on the floor like a baby in her mother's womb, that scripture rescued me. It fed me the life I needed in that moment. And all I could do was pray that Psalms over and over until the fear and rage left.

"The Lord is my light and my salvation, who shall I fear.

The Lord is the strength of my life of whom shall I be afraid.

When the wicked, even my enemies and foes come up against me,

They shall stumble and fall.

Though an army besieges me, my heart will not fear. I shall be confident.

Though my mother and father forsake me, the Lord will receive me."

And then it comforted me. I felt God's peace. It was time to leave.

There are times our spiritual houses are burning down and no one is there to put out the fire. Scripture tells, *"Train up a child in a way they shall go and when he is old, he will not depart."* Proverbs 22:6. There are times when we come to the crossroad between death and life and no one is able to redeem us but God. Have you ever been in a spiritual pit and there is nowhere to run? I am sure we can all relate.

We set out on a quest for joy, love, and peace and one day find our lives plunging into an abyss with no one to deliver us. Our own strength and wisdom has failed us. Our plans seem foolish and our will loses its strength to persevere. It's the darkest night of your soul. You need a miracle, and a miracle fast. You need to know you matter.

It is then we come face to face with our frailty. We realize we cannot depend on ourselves. We need someone greater. We need God.

The pitfall of prostitution, alcoholism, gang violence, domestic violence, human-sex-trafficking, drug addictions, etc., is deep and dark. My pit was deep and dark, filled with rage, depression, bitterness, and self-hatred, but God had granted me a mustard seed of faith and I leaped. I packed my bags with no place to go and that Saturday afternoon I disappeared in the middle of the day across the projects courtyard into the streets of New York City.

RUNAWAY

Running as fast I can,

Never slowing down,

Just in case I was found broken

I was judged the minute I wore my first mini-skirt.

And all the boys on my block stared me down, gave their friends a pound.

She will be my next joint.

I'm 'a smoke her, pass her around and then we will talk about how high we got from her first kiss.

Never thinking for one minute that the little shorty needed a father and it was in their eyes she found this.

And all the women who gossiped didn't know she craved their attention…needed a mother's affection.

They made her famous for being promiscuous.

A runaway,

Running as fast as she can

Never slowing down,

Just in case she was found broken.

RUNAWAY

She became visible.

All eyes on her.

She became the one night stand;

She became the woman no man took home to his mother.

She became the stripper in the club, dancing for a dollar.

She became a married man's lover.

She became the prostitute on the street corner.

She became a baby mother.

She became a wife.

Complicated, and her husband doesn't quite understand why it is so hard to please her.

She became everything just to feel beautiful

She is a runaway.

Running to find her identity, searching for true beauty.

Running. She is a runaway.

Always running,

Never slowing down, just in case she was found broken.

She is a runaway.

I ran out of my father's apartment straight into Marc's arms. On the streets of New York City, Marc became the elixir to my brokenness, only he did not have the capacity to love me unto wholeness. Women with daddy issues eventually end up with men who resemble their fathers.

It did not matter that Marc was a cheater. I stayed. I cooked, cleaned, and answered to his beck and call. He worked, I played wife, just like what I grew up seeing in my home. His love was like broken glass and the longer I held on to his jagged edge, the wider he cut my heart open. It took a fist to my face, a belt whipping, and being locked out of the house in the pouring rain at one in the morning for me to accept he did not love me either. It's a hard pill to swallow when we realize that no one can fix us but God. We make every attempt to fix ourselves and we often look to broken people just like ourselves to do it. The help of people can only take us so far.

We can spend years running here and there looking for love and searching for identity, not realizing that only God is able to speak truth to us and show us who we are in Him. Although he uses people like ourselves to speak, nothing beats the still, quiet voice of the Spirit to remind us who we are. We must not continue running the rat race to gain acceptance by anyone who will dish it out to us. Until we accept God's approval, we will always feel the distress of man's disapproval.

Even when real love comes into our lives, if our system is infected with all kind of emotional viruses, it becomes difficult to fall completely in the arms of love until we surrender to the truth of God's perfect love. Until we have a true conversation with the one who defined and initiated love in the first place, we will continue to grab its shadow.

Psalms 139 has come to be another one of my favorite scriptures. It reminds me that God sees and knows everything about me, even the ruined places. The ruined places are the places in our lives that are torn down like a house being demolished. This place in us is left empty and broken by the workers of destruction in our lives. We tend to run away from the ruined places to avoid shame and ridicule. We are embarrassed by its barrenness, ugliness, and deformity. Even when others discover that we are living in this damaged place, most people don't want to dwell or even visit you there. Human nature loves to dwell in the cleaned and well-furnished places. No one wants to sit in a filthy house with no light. Only God will. God is willing to go where no one else wants to be.

God is in the business of fixing broken things. If there is anywhere Jesus loves to hang out is in broken places. He tends to navigate his way to our shattered dreams, fractured hearts, and desolate selves. God knows us more than anyone else and is willing to stay with us during the dark times. He is our peace in the storm, hope in despair, and light in the dark. To know that no matter where we are God is there should soothe our anxious hearts.

As human beings, it is natural for us to hide the wrecked places from others. We all pack up and run away, but no matter where we run our damaged self goes with us. Although I don't regret the decision to leave my father's, house, I discovered that leaving abusive environments is merely the first step to becoming whole. Healing happens when we hand in our running shoes, sit by the brook of God's word, and drink from the truth.

PSALMS 139

You have searched me, Lord, and you know me.

2 You know when I sit and when I rise;
you perceive my thoughts from afar.

3 You discern my going out and my lying down;
you are familiar with all my ways.

4 Before a word is on my tongue
you, Lord, know it completely.

5 You hem me in behind and before,
and you lay your hand upon me.

6 Such knowledge is too wonderful for me,
too lofty for me to attain.

7 Where can I go from your Spirit?
Where can I flee from your presence?

8 If I go up to the heavens, you are there;
if I make my bed in the depths, you are there.

BEAUTIFUL

9 If I rise on the wings of the dawn,
if I settle on the far side of the sea,

10 even there your hand will guide me,
your right hand will hold me fast.

11 If I say, "Surely the darkness will hide me
and the light become night around me,"

12 even the darkness will not be dark to you;
the night will shine like the day,
for darkness is as light to you.

13 For you created my inmost being;
you knit me together in my mother's womb.

14 I praise you because I am fearfully and wonderfully made;
your works are wonderful,
I know that full well.

15 My frame was not hidden from you
when I was made in the secret place,
when I was woven together in the depths of the Earth.

16 Your eyes saw my unformed body;
all the days ordained for me were written in your book
before one of them came to be.

17 How precious to me are your thoughts, God!
How vast is the sum of them! Were I to count them,
they would outnumber the grains of sand—
when I awake, I am still with you.

From the minute our parents discovered life was on the inside of them, they began the search for the perfect name to give us some form of individuality. We enter into the world and the hunt for identity becomes our quest. In searching for our place in the world, we sometimes encounter the cruelty of others. The world becomes an unsafe place. We discern that man is flawed and this perfect world we fantasize in our heads as children doesn't truly exist. We are forced to accept that people are capable of being wicked, selfish, and unloving, and the only thing that has any power to make perfect is the world inside of us. A dangerous world is a product of people who are dangerous internally.

The only way to navigate this realm despite its fallen nature is to know there is someone greater than ourselves who actually has a map and instructions on how to get where we need to be. Everything ever made has an instruction on how to use it. Because of His love, God provides us a manual. He does not leave us alone. Every good foundation is built and compelled by love.

"For His love is patient, love is kind. It does not envy, it does not boast, it is not proud. It does not dishonor others, it is not self-seeking, it is not easily angered, and it keeps no record of wrongs. His love does not delight in evil but rejoices with the truth. It always protects, always trusts, always hopes, and always perseveres. His love never fails." 1 Corinthians 13:4–7.

It's spiritual. It's surreal. It's supernatural. The everlasting love we yearn for is a divine love that comes only from Heaven, and the only way to experience it, is to spend time in the presence of God through prayer. *"Draw close to me and I will draw close to you."* For it is in His presence we see ourselves the way He sees us, despite the affliction we have experienced. God's love is not just ethereal; it is filled with knowledge and truth. Unlike human love that can be unstable and erratic based on circumstances, God's love stands solid.

It is baffling to comprehend His timeless love because we are blinded by our flaws. Without receiving grace we will always find a way to condemn ourselves, thinking we are not worthy of rescue. Running from our abusers is always the best choice I will tell anyone. If you find a way out, get out. Once you have run, don't hide in other ruined places. Run to the feet of the cross. Run into the arms of truth. Run to the One who heals. Run to the One who keeps the tide within its borders. Run to Him who keeps the Earth on its axis. Run to Him who holds all things together. Run to Him who is able to rebuild, reconstruct, and renew us. God is always in the business of a new you. Let's run straight into the arms of love.

This is where we truly belong.

CHAPTER 14

NO MORE SECRETS

THE GREATEST ENEMY against abuse is the secrets we keep. The secrets of the victim are a deadly poison that seeps into the soul, leaving them helpless, voiceless, and afraid.

Holding the secrets of abuse is like having a wound but being forbidden from telling anyone. Left untreated, the more likely it will become infected. Soon what could have been treated is infected, spreading to other places in the body. It has become detrimental to our health and life. The word "secret" means not to be known or seen by others. Its intent is to be kept confidential and private. Secret places are normally where treasures are kept. Abuse is no treasure; it is a canker worm that eats away at our soul.

"Out of a hundred rapes committed in the United States only thirty-two get reported. Only seven lead to an arrest, and two lead to felony conviction." (Rape, Abuse, and Incest National Network) I can see why victims of abuse chose to stay silent. Besides the unresponsiveness of our legal system, another reason sexually abused victims remain in the shadows is because of shame. Shame is the culprit that keeps us in hiding.

My secret was out, and I had to deal with the consequences.

I became a fighter. I fought for decent meals, fought to graduate high school, fought my way to get a job, fought to go to college, and fought to get an apartment. I fought to stay sane, fought for healthy friendships, and fought to be the woman God wanted me to be. I stayed fighting, and I fought to be me. I became a fighter for the life God promised but there are always obstacles we must overcome in order to truly win. That part of my life as a young adult seemed to be infected with all the wrong men. Men who kissed me then slapped my face. Men who made love to me like I was the only girl in the world then went on to the next girl without looking back. Men to whom I gave my all but they stole valuable parts of me. Men who beat me with their belts to remind me I had no worth. Men who punched me in the ribs to keep me submissive. Men who loved my curves but hated my strength. The men I dated in the past loved me weak. They loved me broken. They loved me dependent. They loved me naked and afraid. They loved me confused. They loved me in every way but myself. I was lost behind my addiction of abusive men and the secrets my family kept. I always knew there was more to the story than what my grandmother disclosed, so one day I bought a ticket and went back to Jamaica to find out the truth.

It had been six years since I saw her last. After leaving my father's house, we lost contact for two years. I didn't call or tell her I was coming to visit her.

When I pulled up to the gate, a neighbor came out to see who I was. Before I finished my sentence the woman clutched my face in her hands, "Jozanne, you Ms. Dixon's granddaughter? She talks about you all the time. Ms. Dixon! Ms. Dixon!" she yelled, running up the stairs.

Mummy came out onto the porch, shocked to see me standing there. Her hair was white and her body frail. I climbed the steps and she embraced me with everything in her. "Welcome home, Jozanne."

Upon entering the house, it was like I had not left. My childhood photos were in the creases of her cabinet and mirrors throughout the house. My old doll Rose Marie was still rocking in the chair as I left her. Overwhelmed by all kinds of emotion, I handed out the gifts I'd brought. Smith was still around and although he and Mummy had finally gotten married, it was simply out of obligation.

I had booked a room at the Pegasus Hotel. The following evening Mummy came to the hotel and we sat on the balcony of the ninth floor outside my room. It was the first time in a long time I looked up in the sky at the stars, and I couldn't help but remember when I believed all things were possible, the world was a safe place, and God was happy with us. I had neither prayed in a while nor set foot in a church. To me, it was useless. I was too far gone from grace.

We sat there quietly. The memory of that abortion clinic still haunted me. As if she could read my mind, Mummy asked me, "What happened between you and your father?" She was ready to have the conversation and I was ready to release my pain. That night I didn't hold back one detail, I spilled all my secrets. It was the most honest I had ever been.

Her face quivered from holding back the tears as I shared all that took place under my father's roof. With a loud outburst, she held her belly and wailed from the balcony. We both wept until we had no tears left.

HER CRY

Her cry groaned unthinkable things
A woman's scorn uprooted
God heard it.
It was a cry for redemption
She wept
A closed chapter to an epic story
A blaze
The fire of secrets
Burned through smoke and mirrors

BEAUTIFUL

God lifted up the truth in his right hand
Nothing was the same that day.
God heard her cry

There on the balcony I laid my head in Mummy's lap while she brushed my hair with her hands. We were ready for the truth and that evening she had the courage to tell me the truth.

JEAN

She was like a delicate lily
Soft, sweet, silent
One of a kind
When she smiled, roses bloomed
And the sun moved
Tender, Eloquent
Mysterious, innocent
The pride of a mother's heart
Handled with a velvet glove
Spotless.
Jean Maureen Ashley
Soft, sweet, and silent

She shared about the day Jean's pale face was burning hot with a fever. Right away, she took her to the town's clinic to see Doctor Brown. Jean followed Doctor Brown into his office while Mummy waited outside. When Dr. Brown returned he had surprising news. Jean was four months pregnant. In disbelief and shame, my grandmother could hardly speak.

Being a sheltered child, it was difficult to accept Jean had a bun in the oven when she did not have a boyfriend. She was only thirteen. She never talked to boys and hardly left the house. Jean was her only daughter and the only gift she felt God gave her. Defensive and disappointed, Mummy yelled across the room, "Jean, Jean, come out here!"

Enraged that her daughter was being looked at as loose girl, Mummy questioned Jean rigorously in front of Dr. Brown. Dr. Brown tried his best to calm Mummy down but she was insistent, "I did not raise her to be a prostitute." Back then, a young girl being pregnant outside of wedlock was a shameful thing.

That night Mummy beat Jean with her brown leather belt, shouting, "What did I tell you? Didn't I tell you not to go to anybody yard? Don't talk to boys. Who is it? Who did dis to you? You have been lying to me all this time?"

Crouched on the floor, Jean explained, "I did not do anything wrong, Mummy."

"Lying lips are an abomination to the Lord. I will kill you in dis house tonight!"

With her leather belt, she gave Jean several lashes across her back. "Tell me the truth! Tell me the truth!"

My grandmother was going to beat the truth out of her daughter that night. Suddenly, Jean blurted out, "Mummy, I don't know his name!"

Astonished by her reply, Mummy held back her belt. "What you mean you don't know his name?"

"It was the day I was late coming home from buying bread. One of the Mcpherson's boys stopped me on the way. I did not stop but when I was coming back, he held my hand. I wanted to leave but he didn't let me go."

Perplexed by this information Mummy pried even more to get some understanding of what Jean was telling her.

HE DIDN'T LET ME GO

He didn't let me go
He didn't let me go
I said NO
But he didn't let me go
My stainless bloom
Hushed under the pillow
Sprung fast
Behind white stained glass doors
Light green walls and concrete floors
Disconnected heartbeat
Beneath bloodstained sheets
Soaked up my tears.
Drowned out by dominoes and Red Stripe beer.
And my virtue disappeared.

As the flickering streetlights rise
I put on my clothes, wiped the tears from my eyes
And came home
I said NO but he didn't let me go.
He didn't let me go, Mummy.

One of the McPhersons' brothers had lured Jean into their blind mother's room and forced himself on her. Hearing this, Mummy's brain could not process it. How could this be possible? She had to put Jean through the wringer a few more times. It was difficult to believe that God allowed something so tragic to befall her precious child. We were talking about *RAPE*. Someone *raped* her daughter. This was also a very shameful act in our community, especially in those days.

NO MORE SECRETS

A woman being raped in our country was and is still a huge taboo. Although most rapists were sought after and killed by the police, a woman is still left with the stigma that she is dirty, useless for another man, and not worthy of marriage. In addition, Jean was pregnant. Back then, a child being pregnant at thirteen years old was basically scorned by society as a whore. This was too much for Mummy to bear.

Later that evening my grandmother, Jean, Jean's dad Derrick, and my grandmother's sister, Pastor Carmen Taylor, paid a visit to the McPhersons' home. All six brothers stood aghast beside their father and blind mother. Mummy asked Jean to point out the culprit who'd ravished her. Timidly, Jean stepped forward and pointed to a twenty-three-year-old Jamaican soldier. He was handsome and dark skinned, with Chinese looking eyes.

"That's him, Mummy, the one with the dimple in his chin," Jean said.

Henry McPherson was his name. He was a cocky soldier, charming, slick in talk, and thought the world owed him something. "I thought she was eighteen," Henry said in his defense.

Derrick charged at him, knocked him to the ground. "You a'go to jail tonight boy!"

All hell broke loose that night. Mummy wanted nothing but revenge for this atrocity committed against her Jeanie.

However, Pastor Carmen Taylor had just about enough of the ruckus between the testosterone in the room. She pulled Mummy to the porch. "Listen, Lorris, I know you guys are angry. Let us not be hasty. Maybe this was a mistake. Let us give this young man the benefit of the doubt," she said calmly.

"This is my one and only child and Henry is not going to get away with this," Mummy fumed.

Pastor Carmen had a more pious outlook on the situation. She reminded Mummy of the importance for a child to have a father, and if she pressed charges, she would be the one to be blame in the long run. "God will make all things beautiful in His time," Pastor Taylor encouraged.

Mummy pondered this a bit because culturally, being a bastard was equally worse in the eyes of most Jamaicans, and neither did she want to offend God. Was it better for Jean to have an abortion, secretly give birth and then give the child away, or should she put Henry McPherson behind bars? Choices. Life is filled with them and sometimes they are extremely difficult to make, especially when we feel we have to live up to the stigma and taboo of a culture. That night Mummy and Jean left defeated without pressing any charges and Henry McPherson was free to go.

Later that evening, Mummy and Jean sat at the dining table. Jean was silent.

"Jeanie, Jeanie, say something. Talk to me," Mummy pleaded. "I am so sorry this happened to you."

Jean remained silent.

"Look, I don't want the neighbors to know about this, do you understand? And you have to take some time off from school."

"Mummy, I want to go to school and play with my friends."

"Don't bring shame to yourself and this house," Mummy responded. "You will stay in this house until it's time to have the baby. Then you can go back to school. No one have to know what happened to you. Just keep your mouth closed."

The shame was too much for Mummy to digest and she kept Jean locked in the house until it was time for her to give birth.

Angry, but too afraid to show it, Jean kept her feelings pent in. Torn between negligence and obedience, she kept silent. No one was coming to her rescue. No one was defending this thirteen year old girl. Once again everyone was more concerned about the opinions of man and how it made *them* appear.

Today, society is still being influenced by the voice of the culture that there is something to feel ashamed of when it comes to rape. Unfortunately, many mothers allow the contempt they feel takes precedent over the justice required to protect their children in these circumstances. This doesn't happen only in Jamaica, but across the world. Young boys and girls are taught consciously or subconsciously that it's their fault why they are maltreated or sexually abused. Rarely does the perpetrator suffer any consequences for their action. From childhood to adulthood, many rape victims are left to battle the emotional journey on their own. This uphill battle becomes years of emotional, psychological, physical, and sexual trauma.

For nine months Jean stayed locked away in the house to avoid the ridicule of the community. Her voice was silenced, her beauty marred, and her power stripped until it was time to deliver her unwanted baby.

Mummy rushed Jean to Jubilee Hospital on September 5, but ironically, there was nothing to be jubilant about. For twenty-seven hours Jean hollered from the excruciating pain of an undeveloped uterus trying push out an eight-and-a-half-pound baby.

PUSH

Five months later
Twenty-four hours of labor pain

PUSH

Push, little girl, they said
Push real hard
We can see the head

Five months later,
Twenty-four hours of labor pain

PUSH

BEAUTIFUL

Push, little girl, they said
Push through the fear
Push through the shame

PUSH

Her inward part torn
Her childhood scorned
The struggle in her womb
Life wanted to be born

PUSH, little girl
Just...PUSH

The nurse cut the umbilical cord and handed Jean her gift, but she turned her face away. Mummy picked the child up in her arms. Neither knew what to do with this new life, but they had no choice. I was here in this world and everyone had to deal with it.

Like a ripped sheet, the nurses stitched Jean's vagina up and a week later she was released to go home. Mummy tried to adjust, but felt a load of guilt about her decision to keep hushed about the situation. She prayed for things to go back to normal, but there was now a broken thirteen year old child, a regretful grandmother, and a baby no one really wanted.

My dad stopped by weekly out of obligation to drop off some milk and a few dollars to compensate for his iniquitous conscience. He tried stirring up conversation with Jean and she pretended to be happy just to appease her mother.

Truth be told, however, no one gets a pass on deception by brushing it under the rug. Mummy made every effort to fix things, but Jean had something brewing inside of her. Her silence became haunting and her behavior bizarre. One day Mummy caught Jean cutting the pubic hair on her private part. When she asked her why, Jean replied, "This way a man won't like it." Perplexed, Mummy made every effort to withhold the rain, but the clouds never cleared, and one night it stormed at 33 Giltress Avenue.

I was turning one year old when my dad came by with news that he had gotten a visa to visit his sister in America. He promised Mummy he was staying only for three weeks. At first Mummy was skeptical, but going to America was a huge deal to all Jamaicans. In the back of her mind she thought this would be a great opportunity for us all.

Henry left and three weeks turned into months, and then years. No one knew when he was planning to return. That year my father left, Jean became more withdrawn and her behavior more peculiar, especially in the middle of the night. She would get up in the middle of the night and stare at me in the crib.

"Jean what's wrong? Go to bed. It's late," Mummy said from the doorway. Jean did not respond. This went on almost every night around midnight.

Yet nothing compared to one specific night when Jean could not sleep. The day before, she seemed depressed and fatigued. After dinner around 6:30 p.m. she was sorrowful and the tears began to flow. Mummy did everything to console her, but Jean did not stop crying. The clock turned midnight and Jean was still crying. Terrified and feeling helpless, Mummy left her alone so she could get some sleep. That night, Jean's tears went from deep sorrow to uncontrollable rage.

IN THE MIDDLE OF THE NIGHT

In the middle of the night
In the middle of the night
She yearned to be a child again.
She hated the womb that carried her
She hated the womb inside of her
Her soul grieved

BEAULIFUL

Her heart ached
In the middle of the night
In the middle of the night
Her silence grew louder
She disappeared behind a baby's cry
Her breast milk turned sour
Her seething storm
Needed the hands of God
To quiet rage being born
In the middle of the night
In the middle of the night.
She looked in the mirror
Her reflection snickered
Her mind played tricks
It was her baby's fault why she was sick
In the middle of the night.

And in the middle of the night, she charged into my room, picked me up from the crib, carried me to the porch, and threw me into the yard. Running down the steps screaming, Mummy picked up an unconscious baby she was certain had died. "Jean! Jean! What have you done to your baby?" Jean stood on the porch with a smirk on her face, as if she had gained victory over the thing that had caused her so much shame. Like a raging lion, Jean stormed through the house breaking every glass and mirror. The harder Mummy try to calm her down, the more furious she became.

That night two ambulances came to our house. One to take me to Children's Hospital and the other to take Jean to Bellevue Hospital. My grandmother watched from the gate as her shy and quiet child became a fuming, confrontational tyrant.

"Get off me, Get off me! I hate you, Mummy. I hate you!" Jean screamed as two paramedics restrained her.

Jean unleashed her fury on whoever was available to take it. Devastated, Mummy waved goodbye to her daughter that night and got in the ambulance with me. That was the moment my grandmother became my Mummy.

That night under the stars on the balcony of Pegasus Hotel, the truth was revealed about how I came into the world and what kind of man my father was. It was incomprehensible to try to understand how one man had destroyed three women's lives. Torn between outrage and empathy as to why my grandmother handed me over to a man who could not be trusted, I sat there quietly and held my peace. As disturbing as it was, it all made sense why we were here in this station.

Those secrets had us living in the shadows. Trying to cover everyone's lies had us making foolish decisions. The secrets did not help us one bit, only made everything worse, taking us on roads with dead ends. No life came from our secrets. No good to celebrate. No reasons to praise God. We had lived in this shame, afraid of what everyone else thought. We thought our secrets could protect us, and instead they had destroyed us.

That day on the balcony, I made a decision to start a new chapter in my life. The truth gave clarity and direction. Sometimes we think not knowing the truth will make life easier but what it actually does is give you permission to move on. When the truth is exposed, it is God's divine moment to grant you the freedom you always wanted. It will hurt. It will make you cry and it will feel uncomfortable, but the truth will always make us free.

The trip came to an end, and so did another chapter of my life. Heading back to the United States with the secrets out lifted the weight I carried all those years. This was my opportunity to change the narrative.

Seize the moment.

CHAPTER 15

RETURNING TO LOVE

THE JOURNEY OF life can be filled with dead ends and detours. We lose our way from the original plan and purpose God ordained for our lives. These obstacles challenge our faith and leave us disoriented about who we are. We forget that we were once loved and treasured by a good God. There is something about knowing the truth and accepting it. The revelation behind my mother's illness motivated me to search for a better life. I became determined to not allow the past define my future. It became quite imperative to discover who I was before I became a reflection of my parents.

My only weapon of warfare was prayer. I had now found myself on the upper West Side, kept by a wealthy French man who was old enough to be my father. Although he had the money to splurge on me, the truth was it was time to stand on my two feet, and become the woman God created.

From my window looking over the Hudson River, I did the only thing I knew to do, ask God for help. "Lord, help me." The prayer was neither complex nor eloquent with fancy theological jargon. It came from the depths of my heart. So often we think we have to be spiritually adorned in perfection to come to the throne of grace. We feel mucky and ashamed to utter a word to God, and we shy away from His love. We say "God can't fix us," or "God won't fix us."

Truthfully, God doesn't need a long prayer. Nor does He need us to come to Him perfect. *"He knows what we need before we even say it."* Matthew 6:8. No matter where we are or who we are, God will meet us in our mess. Perfection is never a requirement to approach our Maker. He bends His ears to our cry, He judges not our iniquities, and He is never shocked at what we tell Him. He delights in our humility and has compassion in our brokenness.

My prayer went straight to God's ears and a few weeks later the rich Frenchman told me, *"I will pay your rent and utilities for one year until you get yourself on your feet."* He placed five hundred dollars on the table to take care of my basic needs for the rest of the month and left. God had done a miracle. We may think miracles are signs and wonders, where limbs grow on a broken leg or a dead man comes to life. However, God performs miracles every day, and they mostly come in the simplest deeds, like a hug, a helping hand, or a smile. We all need something to remind us that God cares and it is does not always come with fanfare. Every one of us can be a sign and a wonder to each other by showing acts of kindness and love.

There is nothing greater than when we know our father in Heaven hears us. We may find ourselves in sticky situations, where we are unable to get out. But is there any situation that God can't pull us out from? *"I am the LORD, the God of all mankind. Is anything too hard for me?"* Jeremiah 32:27. It delights His heart to know we believe in His amazing love. Nothing pleases a father's heart more than knowing his daughter or son trusts him. We must not allow our abusive pasts to rob us of a new life. Regardless of our circumstances, our Heavenly father's character is trustworthy and dependable. Wherever we are, whatever our situation, stand by, because any minute He will show Himself as faithful.

Within a year I bought a one way ticket to Southern California, and things began to fall in place. I got signed to my first agent and starred in my first national commercial. When we take away the clutter from our mental space, our minds become the resident where God's dream abides and we thrive. God's plans are perfect and nothing can prevent them from going forth once we are following the leading of His Spirit.

Coming to Los Angeles was where I came to myself. Just like the prodigal son who had left his father's house. The Bible says, *"When he came to his senses, he said, 'how many of my father's hired servants have food to spare, and here I am starving to death! I will set out and go back to my father and say to him: Father, I have sinned against Heaven and against you. I am no longer worthy to be called your son.' So he got up and went to his father. But while he was still a long way off, his father saw him and was filled with compassion for him; he ran to his son, threw his arms around him and kissed him. But the father said to his servants, 'Quick! Bring the best robe and put it on him. Put a ring on his finger and sandals on his feet. Bring the fattened calf and kill it. Let's have a feast and celebrate."* Luke 15:17–23.

Sometimes we forget who God created us to be and we find ourselves living in places not fit for a princess. In order to see the amazing plan God has for our lives we must get off the drama train and refresh our acquaintance with Him. It is in the surrender we discover God's original plan for our lives. Just like the prodigal son, one Sunday morning I walked into West Angeles Church. God's arms were wide open to receive this broken vessel. The warm smiles of the ushers at the front door reminded me that I was not forgotten. That morning when the pastor preached a message of hope, living water washed my soul in the back pew. Each word from the pulpit pulled on my heart. I had returned to love, not church, not ministry, not religion. The words spoken were life and it was imparted in my soul by the spirit. This was not new love, it was a love lost. It was true love. This love made sense. It was clear, peaceful, and fulfilling. It had no burdensome demands; it was not manipulative and difficult. It was honest, patient, simple, and breathtaking.

The world had taken pieces of me and all my idols had shown themselves to be nothing but an illusion. No one knew how to love me with all my imperfections, or knew how to love me to whole-ness. But it was clear that day God loved me. My past was irrelevant. He wanted all of me, the good, the bad, and the ugly. I was a lady of many secrets and too many unholy encounters to mention. That Sunday morning God called me by name and life was never the same. *"For those he predestined, he also called; those he called, he also justified; those he justified, he also glorified."* Romans 8:30. He is all you need.

When God calls us it's not a long drawn out speech, it is right *now*. It is not religion, or a church made by man's hands. It is the way life was meant to be. His word spoken to us is full of life. It is going back to the beginning where we once knew we were loved. He begins to detail our lives with His Word, celebrate us with His blessings, and open our minds to all He created us to be.

This was the beginning of a new life for me. I was learning to be dependent on the Creator for everything I needed It was the first time I was alone with God. To have a love encounter spending time alone with God is necessary. The best person to deliver a love message is God. *"God's thoughts of us outweigh the number of sand."* Just imagine not spending time with the person who loves you. How would you know their thoughts of you? When we respond to love, it ultimately reacquaints us with who we are and who God is. It is in the secret place where we hear His voice clearly and He gives us direction for our lives.

Jesus' daily practice was to spend quality time with his Heavenly father. *"Very early in the morning, while it was still dark, Jesus withdrew to a solitary place to be alone with God and pray."* Mark 1:35. Jesus spent the majority of his time with God. Before many of His miracles, you will discover Jesus went away with God. Jesus knew His lifeline was connected to the father and there was nothing He could do apart from Him.

Spending time with God in prayer is where we learn to live and love again. When we return to love, we must drop everything that hinders our relationship with Him. It's there we get to know the truth and start on the journey to our true destiny.

We are all capable of moving forward, regardless how unbearable and impossible it looks. God will show us He is more than able. My good friend Dalia once told me, "Don't give up five minutes before your miracle." Most times, we do. We throw in the towel, leave the boxing ring defeated, and never lift a hand to give the devil a black eye. If you want to give the devil a black eye, run to the prayer closet, get on your knees, and cry out to God.

The thoughts in my head told me "You are nothing," "You will never make it," and "You are broken, filthy, and have no worth." It was a constant barrage from an enemy unwilling to retreat. However, we can't carry this baggage for the rest of our lives. It is impossible to love the new you when the old you gets permission to speak. Our biggest challenge ahead is saying goodbye to the past. Past pain has no good thing to offer our present or future self. When we abide every day in the promises of God, it helps us to overcome the past. Returning to love takes daily practice. It takes seeking, knocking, and asking.

This is where identity is established. Every creation was thought through, planned out, and executed by its inventor. It takes enormous intelligence to design a human being. That being the case, it is of maximum importance to know the One who took the time to design and to know for what purpose.

Purpose. Every human desires it, questions it, and needs it. It is the drive and reason for everything we do. When we find it, it changes everything about us. However, finding purpose does not come easily. Purpose will take time alone with God. It is not cheap. It will cost us everything. It humbles us, strips us of the misconceived ideas of who we think we are. It shifts us and ultimately it will transform us. If none of these things are happening, we must reconsider the path. Purpose takes asking and seeking spiritual things to understand who we are inside these jars of clay. Purpose is a response to love.

For four years I sought God relentlessly, and I am not talking about church attendance. The disposition of my heart was to seek God in everything and see Him in all things. This led me one day to go on a forty day fast at a small church in the city of Gardena, California.

It was time to get away from all the noise and distraction. I wanted to know who I was and why I was born. The church was used for hosting missionaries and housing the homeless. With only a few clothes I embarked on this spiritual pilgrimage. This was one of the most radical decisions I had ever made in my faith walk. A few of my peers thought I was losing my mind, which is often the response when God calls us to a faith walk. We come off as strange and erratic, irrational and peculiar. No one understands you. You don't make sense. That's when it makes all the sense in the world. In order to know who we are, we need to take the unpredictable road. It actually feels like when you first fall in love. It actually does not make sense. You can't stop thinking of the person, there is nothing you would not do for them. You break all your rules just to accommodate your newfound love. Everyone says to you, "You are different." Love will do that.

When God calls us, he calls us in the most unconventional ways. He rarely calls in convenience and it will take faith to follow him wholeheartedly. It is a response to love. King Solomon said, *"Love is as strong as death."* He is correct. Love is not for the faint of heart, nor is fulfilling our destiny. It will cost us everything.

This reminds me of Mary, the mother of Jesus. Here was a young woman who was betrothed and God decided she would carry the Messiah. Today we look at this story with great honor, yet this honorable event came with great sacrifice and responsibility. For a young girl around the age of fourteen years old to have such a huge calling, it shows us that God does not discriminate when it comes to age or gender. Mary did not request this visitation; she was *chosen* for it. Just like us. We all are chosen for a specific purpose and are rarely qualified for the work, but God has already justified us for the task. Mary had to deal with explaining the unexplainable: "You did not have sex and you are pregnant? Yeah, okay, Mary."

I am sure people in her neighborhood were gossiping, not to mention her fiancé, Joseph. What in the world was *he* thinking? *"Mary done messed around and now she's making up stories."* The calling of God will bring judgment and sometimes ridicule. Hence, the cross. I am sure Joseph was wondering how Mary got pregnant when he had not known her in that way. Listen, when God call us, it normally baffles everyone around us. Mary was called at a time when she seemed not equipped and qualified. Yet God wanted her to participate in this world-changing event.

What I love about Mary was she did not run from her assignment. *"Be it unto me as you have said oh, God,"* was her response. As we all know, answering her assignment came with lots of trials and tribulations. Mary would one day lose her most precious gift in a horrendous way that no mother should have to bear. Her obedience to God brought many tears and pierced her soul. But her pain brought healing to the world. After all that weeping, one day Mary was going to leap for joy when she witnesses her son ascending into the heavens. Just like for Mary, our deepest pain doesn't have to leave us bitter, angry, and hopeless. Weeping will endure for the night but joy will come in the morning.

There I was sitting in a little church, not a penny to my name. No phone, no agent, no friends. Nothing. There was nothing in my life to distract me from His voice. During those forty days, I poured out my heart to the Lord and in the midst of it all I realized that although I was resurrected from the dead, the grave clothes of unforgiveness was still in my heart. Don't you hate it when you think you know yourself, only to discover you are simply at the tip of the iceberg?

I was lying on my back in the intercessory prayer room, my heart burdened with many questions about the future. Although I wasn't sure what I was waiting for, I needed something that would change my life and shift the paradigm of my thoughts. Then twelve days into the fast when love walked into the room. The brightest light I had ever seen entered. It hovered over me and my inner being expanded as if it was larger than the vessel in which it resides. The presence of His glory left me in awe and all I could do was utter His name. Jesus. Jesus! Love walked into the room and embraced me. His love was unexplainable, yet truthful. Nothing I had ever experienced compared to His love. In that moment, His love erased everything I had been through. My Earthly parents were irrelevant, material things were not a thought, my pain did not exist. All I could see and feel was Him. All I wanted was Him. His presence stayed with me for what felt like a lifetime, though I am sure it was for a short moment.

I was His desire. He wanted me relentlessly. I belonged to Him and everything in my being knew it. It was not a strange phenomenon. I knew Him and He knew me. My soul knew Him. He quenched my thirst and filled me up with an overflow of love and joy that could not be contained. He wanted me more than anyone and all my soul longed for was Him. He was passionate for me. I was precious to Him. Speechless and in awe, I surrendered to His love. Yes, God was enough. He wanted to show me that everything I needed was in Him. True love does exist and it begins with God. I knew then that no matter what I achieved in the future, nothing compared to the love of God.

Everything about His presence spoke love. There was no judgment, no fear, no accusation, and no shame. His love was not of this world. I was spotless. My sins were not mentioned once nor those of anyone who sinned against me. I stared into His eyes only for a moment and instantly I was captivated. His love is a consuming fire, not the kind that burns but the kind that yearns for us to be one with Him. God's love takes us from glory to glory. It pulls us out and up. The energy, the vibrancy, the frequency. Heaven had surely invaded Earth. This was the affirmation I needed to help me cross over to the next stage of my life. *"Come away with me, my beloved,"* was his love language. He loved me from the inside out, demanded all of me, and I was ready to give my life to Him. This experience has changed me forever.

This new life I was experiencing was different. It was filled with love, power, and peace. It was feeling the Father's love for the first time in my life. I had no desire to be validated by anyone. It was truly the peace that surpassed all understanding. The constant cycle of desiring a male figure to fulfill an absent father was no longer required. It was a dying to the world and the affections of it. I am not saying I needed no one or nothing material. We all need people, fellowship, a place to live, food, etc. I am saying the desire to have someone in my life I held responsible for my peace, joy, and happiness vanished. I had come to the place where I learned to love God, and love myself *in* God.

When we encounter true love, it forces us to reciprocate with love. God's love compels us to love ourselves and love others. Encounters with God will transform us. We begin to see through His eyes rather through the lens of our abuse. Personally, I became more sensitive to the Spirit of God. I became more compassionate and less indifferent. I wanted to serve more than receive. My heart became more open and free, like when I was a child. My spirit was vibrant like the four year old girl with that one wheel cart. Everything was possible. In addition, I began to attract not creepy, abusive men, but men who respected and adored me. It is true that when we change, everything around us changes. We attract who we are and we tolerate with what resonate. Love is the most powerful spiritual experience in the world and when it happens, it heals and sets free.

We can only return to love when we return to God. When we do, we literally become born again. We are transformed into a new person spiritually. We become a reflection of Heaven and resemblance of Christ, who is a true example of love.

Beautiful, God is always ready to celebrate our homecoming. Yes, you have been away for a while. Yes, some horrible things have happened to you. Yes, you have squandered all the precious places in you on those who did not recognize your worth. But it is never too late. *"For I am the LORD your God, who upholds your right hand, who says to you, 'Do not fear, I will help you.'"* Isaiah 41:13. Run to His loving arms. Let Him clothe you in righteousness and caress you with His everlasting love. He awaits your arrival.

It's never too late.

CHAPTER 16

GOD IS ENOUGH

A PASTOR ONCE told me, "You can have as much of God as you want." I wanted all of who God is. Although God was gracious in giving me the desires of my heart and fulfilling some of my dreams, these pursuits of happiness never brought me any true peace. The novelties of success are generally short lived and we are off to the next pursuit. Now don't get me wrong, there is nothing wrong in pursuing the goals aligned with your destiny.

In the midst of success it's imperative that we pursue wholeness as well. The material things of the world will not compensate for our brokenness. We live in a world where pain and turmoil is inevitable. As long as we are on this Earth, no one bypasses heartbreak. But the faith walk helps us overcome our adversity. In pursuing God, we realize that not only is He enough, *we* are enough. We discover that we are greater than our afflictions.

Our experiences, both good and bad, are here to teach us who we are and why we are here. The biggest misconception is that we lack something when God gave us everything. That everything is not material. It is a place of spiritual abundance that enables us to live victoriously even when faced with tragedy. When we acknowledge that God is sufficient, we will find fulfillment internally, and we will never lose sight of who we are. *"Anyone who listens to the word but does not do what it says is like someone who looks at his face in a mirror and, after looking at himself, goes away and immediately forgets what he looks like.*" James 1:23. A person can have the whole world and still feel empty. Dreams can be fulfilled and yet we are not satisfied. Even if we were immensely wealthy, we can still be spiritually bankrupt. Why is that? Forgive me, but I tend to ask questions because it allows us to use our brain and dig for truth. What is the point of life? Why are you here? Why all the pain? Is it just to torture us? Are we merely puppets on a string for God's amusement?

Those questions took me on a quest for truth during those forty days. After that experience, the blessings came, and so did the test. I met an amazing Nigerian man named Sunday who became my life partner. A new chapter was beginning in my life. This relationship was different. It was not co-dependent, abusive, or futile. It had purpose, love, and honor.

We made plans for a small, intimate wedding with only a few friends and the preacher. It was going to be an unconventional wedding with an African theme. The list was being checked off, from who would be my maid of honor to the fufu we were going to serve at the reception. Everything was planned perfectly until ten days before my wedding when I realized I had not chosen anyone to give me away. Although there were amazing men in my life I could have called to do the honors, it never crossed my mind.

Wrestling with the thought over and over in my head, I felt the need to call my father. This was a crazy and a farfetched thought. Not sure whether it was a thought ignited by emotionalism or by the spirit, I prayed and sought the Lord again. Picking up the phone and calling a man I had not spoken with in almost ten years was more than ridiculous, it was foolish. After all he had done to me and the disaster he left in my life, he was the last person deserving my presence, especially during one of the most significant turning points of my life, my wedding.

After much contemplation, the Spirit spoke to me. *"Call your father and honor him."* You know I wanted to rebuke the devil. Isn't it like us to run in the other direction when God speaks a word that doesn't agree with our flesh? But it was not the Devil; it was the lover of my soul, breathing into me His nature. A love encounter will do that. That night God made it clear that in order for me to be free from my past, it was important to forgive my Earthly father for all he had done to me. My pride counseled me, "He is not worth it." He was dishonorable. He did not deserve my affection, love, or even pity. Yet God wanted me to cast all that was good on a man most people would not consider "good."

The following morning I called my dad. While I waited, those three rings felt like a hundred rings, and then he answered. The lump in my throat I felt as a little girl came right back. There was silence on the phone for a while until I stuttered, "D-Dad I am getting m-married in ten days, and I would like for you to attend my w-wedding." I could not believe the words coming out of my mouth.

"Why?" he asked.

I had no idea. I did not know why I was doing this, I only knew I was led to do it.

When the Spirit speaks, we don't always get an answer why, we simply need to obey. Our answer comes in the obedience. I waited for my father's reply, but he said he needed more time to think about it. We hung up and I stepped outside to catch my breath. It was a sunny day and the palm trees swayed, reminding me of Jamaica and my grandmother. I sat on the porch thinking, *"You are such a fool. Everyone in your family will say, 'She is liar.' Why call your father if he had done those things to you?"* I was long past caring what my family thought about me. I was no longer an abused little ten year old girl, I was a woman who had become secure in my identity and now was living on purpose.

Unsure whether or not he was coming, there was no other choice but to leave the outcome in God's hand. Whether he attended or not, God was going to give me an answer one way or the other. Finally my dad responded that he was planning to attend. After all these years, I was going to face the man who had brought me close to death. There was no plan or rehearsed speech. I needed to trust Jesus every step of the way. God will ask of us the unimaginable and the only action left for us is to walk by faith. In those times we don't need to worry about what we should say, just trust that God will give us what we need at the appropriate time.

Two days before my wedding, my father and I met at a Starbucks. Like two strangers we sat across from each other waiting for the right moment to speak. Broken, there we were looking to each other for some solace. Finally I had the courage to ask, "Why did you do those things to me as a child?"

"Lust," he told me. *Lust.* That one word had much depth. I understood that lust, when it is full grown, can be powerful and take a grip on our lives. It's just like anything else, the lust for alcohol, drugs, sex. We find ourselves doing things we don't want to do.

It's a place where we feel incapable of stopping. We want to but we enjoy the momentary gratification no matter how sick and demented it is. Although we know it is wrong, we can't help ourselves. It feeds our need to have control or power. We become addicted, wondering why we can't shake it. That is because it is tied to our spiritual self. Sex and love, just like food, is a natural need.

Before I go further, I know some of you will say "please don't compare pedophilia to drug and alcohol addictions."

Please, hear me out for a minute. All things given to man can be misused. A person who can't stop eating has a deeper need than food. They hide food under their bed, violate their conscience for food, and are incapable of stopping. Drugs are the same thing. I have counseled drug addicts and in the midst of our conversation that person will look me in the eyes and tell me they are not high, even though it is clear they are on drugs. That person will lie, steal, and hurt anyone just to get a fix. The same goes for sex. Some men will cheat on their wives, some are addicted pornography, and others prey on the innocent.

GOD IS ENOUGH

That day as I sat across from the man I thought I could not live without, I finally had the courage to confront him about the molestation and how much havoc it caused in my life. He didn't interrupt, but listened carefully. After I was finished, he said, "I am sorry." I could not see his eyes behind the green tinted shades but I saw the tears. Then he said it again. "I am sorry." I sat there speechless, thinking after ten years, all he could say was, "I am sorry." I didn't know what to say. His apology was not enough to console me, nor was it enough to heal me. But God's love and grace was sufficient for both of us.

As if the Holy Spirit walked into that café, I felt His presence—grace and love. My eyes filled to the brim with tears because I was a benefactor of that grace. Grace means we are undeserving, yet God still shows His favor. It means compared to God's standard, which is perfect in love, we fall short, yet God lavishes His love on us regardless of the disposition of our hearts.

I previously had an encounter with God and now God was asking me to return the favor. I knew love erases everything, and if God was willing to forgive me, I was capable of forgiving others for what they had done to me. Getting familiar with God's presence is one of the most powerful things we can do. It's in His presence yokes are broken. It's in His presence healing takes place. It's in His presence old things become new and dead things come alive. No one can claim a sinless life and that is why the grace of God is life transforming. God's presence is necessary for transformation. Keep in mind, His presence and the way He speaks does not have to be the same for everyone. He has a unique relationship with every single person. He is personable and intentional, like a father who has two children; each of them has a separate relationship but He is still the same person. What I am saying, is you don't need to go on a forty day fast to find God, nor do you need to have my experience, but I am sure when you seek with all your heart, He will reveal Himself to *YOU*! It will be unique, relevant, and life transforming, specifically catered for you and your assignment.

The Lord wanted me to extend grace to my father, right in that moment. Not later, but right there in Starbucks. Yes, Grace is *now*. Love is now! It is instant. It is merciful. It is willing to completely take us from darkness to light in seconds. It is faster than the speed of light. It has no boundaries. It lavishes on everything it touches and it was now my time to extend it to someone I thought seemed most unworthy.

"All have sinned and fallen short of the glory of God." Romans 3:23. Thank God that He sent His only begotten son to show us the way. He was so passionate for us; He gave His best offering to win our hearts. If we look back at Jesus' life, we see that His ministry began in a lake of sinners, the minute He humbled Himself so John the Baptist could baptize him. Jesus needed no salvation. He was without sin, so why did He find it pertinent to be baptized with sinners? I believe it was God's way to show he shared in our suffering. To take it further, when Jesus' ministry ended, He was crucified between two thieves. Even at the point of death, Jesus was still able to forgive. This shows God's heart for those who commit unmentionable sin. God's greatest gift to mankind is forgiveness in the expression of Jesus Christ and one of the greatest gifts we can give to another person is forgiveness. True forgiveness is not dependent on anything. It extends its hand, seeking no response, no results. It doesn't need consolation or reconciliation. If love was a plant, forgiveness would be the root.

I know what you are thinking: *How can we forgive a man who has committed all these atrocities? And how can God forgive the sins of the world? Wars. Murders. Injustices. Exploitations of the poor.* You name it, I ask the same thing. How can God forgive the sins of the world? Love is the answer. Forgiveness is the most radical expression of love and redemption to our healing. It helps the person who needs the forgiveness, yet it saves the victim from being held captive in their own pain that comes with unforgiveness. It gets rid of bitterness. It removes anger, and most importantly, it restores them.

GOD IS ENOUGH

Some of the problems we have in our personal lives stem from the heart of unforgiveness. Forgiveness is expensive, and that is why we rarely give it. Forgiveness is not an overnight, manmade emotion. It is a supernatural experience that only comes from above. Jesus was and still is the greatest example of forgiveness. Forgiveness takes us fighting for our hearts to be renewed with love gain. Forgiveness takes prayer and meditation. It takes everything we possess to grant it to someone. When Jesus forgave, it was not with words. He was crushed, beaten, and ridiculed. It took his life to forgive. Forgiveness will also cost you. The life of Jesus shows us the way to forgiveness. Forgiveness never makes us feel good at first. We feel foolish, humbled, and crushed.

However, forgiveness does not say we are weak or foolish. Instead, it reveals who we are. It reveals once again our identity that we are greater than our experiences. Deep inside of our spiritual DNA is the capacity to love and heal supernaturally. We are all capable of God's love. We are stronger than our pain. We are not our bodies. We are powerful way beyond what we think and feel. Our lives can reveal the nature of God if we allow Him to work within our hearts. Forgiveness takes us from below and positions us at the right hand of the Father. Forgiveness gives us dominion over evil. Forgiveness is the last thing we want to lavish on anyone when they have wronged us. Yet forgiveness should be the first thing we seek out in order to be healed. I know someone may have hurt you and caused much harm to your soul, but I encourage you to take a leap of faith and offer forgiveness in your own way. I promise you, you will not regret it. Forgiveness ultimately leads us to the path that God is enough and we are enough in Him.

My heart was circumcised and the residue of my callous heart disappeared. The hatred and the anger vanished. It was in that moment I had a glimpse of eternity when Jesus spoke three words: "It is finished." It *was* finished. My heart was no longer a captive of my past. The act of forgiveness is the currency of our freedom. This is the power of the cross. *"Father forgive them because they know not what they do." "But he was pierced for our transgressions, he was crushed for our iniquities; the punishment that brought us peace was on him, and by his wounds we are healed."* Isaiah 53:4. The cross is the most powerful spiritual revelation. It does not merely save us, it gives us a new life.

One of my favorite scriptures is in Philippians 4:6–9: *"Be anxious for nothing but in everything, by prayer and petition, with thanksgiving, present your requests to God. And the peace of God, which transcends all understanding, will guard your hearts and your minds in Christ Jesus. Finally, brothers, whatever is true, whatever is noble, whatever is right, whatever is pure, whatever is lovely, whatever is admirable—if anything is excellent or praise worthy—think on about such things. Whatever you have learned or received or heard from me, or seen in me, put it into practice. And the God of peace will be with you."*

When we forgive it forces our thoughts to only think on the goodness of God. We have made it to the other side. *"Oh, bless the Lord Oh my soul. You open your hand and satisfy the desire of every living thing. The LORD is righteous in all His ways and kind in all His deed."* Psalms 145:16–17. The prolific evangelist Beth Moore once said, *"With God, you can be in the fire and come out not smelling like smoke."* We do not have to look like what we have been through.

We cannot stay so stuck in the past that we can't grab hold of what God is doing now. We must not allow life to pass us by and rob us of precious moments. Unforgiveness is our worst enemy to our healing. It is the place where we live over and over the atrocity of another's sinful action towards us. It keeps us bound to the wound and torments our soul through the spirit of anger, bitterness, and resentment. It judges, condemns, and soon enough it hates. We know what hate does. It murders the individual who has done us wrong over and over and over in our hearts.

Unforgiveness is a spiritual bacterium. Like cancer, it slowly creeps in, and eventually shuts our entire system down. We die spiritually. The scriptures said, *"For God has come to give us life and life more abundantly,"* and one of the main ways He gives life is through forgiveness. Every person, no matter the sin, no matter the rejection of God, God has forgiven them through giving the ultimate sacrifice, His Son, Jesus Christ. In our carnal minds that does not make a lick of sense. It's inconceivable, but it is God's power of salvation.

God wanted me to experience the ultimate sacrifice, which was to give the most precious part of my life to someone who was undeserving in most people's eyes. Some people I am sure called me a fool, but sometimes God uses the foolish things of this world to shame the wise. The oppression, heaviness, and pain we feel is not just a result of someone hurt, it is most times the unwillingness to forgive.

This was my moment to forgive, and by faith I took the opportunity. On my wedding day, my dad walked me down the aisle. My groom stood there in his splendor, waiting for his bride. Our guests, draped in African raiment, rose to their feet as I walked down the aisle with my father. Most of the people did not know all that had taken place. Everyone cheered, smiled, and blessed us. Isn't it like Jesus to give the best part of himself to those who did not deserve it? He takes us as His bride and presents us to His father regardless of all we have done. He invites us to the wedding, allowing us to feast and partake of Him.

The greatest solution to every complex problem is in the wisdom of God. He is the only one who can add a positive to a negative and make it a positive. He is the only one who uses the dilemma of our lives to bring us to our destiny. His love is confounding. That day I received a new name, as well as a new heart. The ties that once held me bound were severed forever. Isn't God marvelous!

When we freefall into the hands of our Creator, He catches us and molds us into His perfect image. My father walking me down the aisle changed me completely. It was a mission I was incapable of carrying out without the Lord's help but it was one of the best decisions in my life. Forgiveness buries our past and arrays our future with infinite possibilities. We are more than abused, broken, and shameful. We are God's beautiful brides. We are seated in Heavenly places, crowned with precious jewels of peace, joy, and love.

Beloved, no matter where we have been or what we've been through, we must never allow unforgiveness to keep us from living our lives. Keep in mind that weight is anything that impedes motion, and trust, me unforgiveness weighs *a ton*. When we extend forgiveness to those who have caused us great pain, freedom awaits us. My pastor, Holly Wagner, shared at She Rises one of the most profound statements: "Forgiveness does not excuse their behavior. Forgiveness prevents their behavior from destroying your heart." Beloved, God is more than enough and you can have as much of Him as you desire. Extend forgiveness and receive your freedom.

You are greater than our pain.

A PRAYER OF FORGIVENESS

Lord, thank you for your forgiveness.

Today I choose to walk in forgiveness.

I release _____ from the anger and hatred I have in my heart.

I forgive_____.

I forgive their abusive actions.

I forgive their lack of love and the pain it has caused in my life.

I forgive their absence and unrepentant heart towards the damages they left in my spiritual house.

I forgive _____.

And God, not only do I forgive _____,

Today I let go of toxic behaviors as a result of my abuse.

Forgive me for recklessly crossing over into love when there was a flashing red light that told me danger was ahead.

Forgive me for handing my heart to those who told me by their actions I had had no value, yet I granted them the best of me.

GOD IS ENOUGH

Forgive me for revealing my nakedness when love and honor was not in the room.

Forgive me for being impatient on basking in your presence so I can recognize you in others.

Forgive me for blaming others for my mistakes when your grace always gave me another chance.

Forgive me for believing everyone's definition of me when you told me the truth.

Forgive me for holding onto past hurt, when you granted me the keys to freedom.

Forgive me for allowing bitterness to take root in my heart, when your spirit is sweeter than honey.

Forgive me, Lord, for my unbelief when the truth of your word gives me liberty and I am unwilling to free myself.

Forgive me of my unbelief and grant me the faith that will move mountains.

Lord, right now I choose to live in the place where forgiveness dwells and grant it to _____.

I am grateful for your gentleness to walk with me through this process and I receive your grace to accomplish this task.

Thank you for freedom and thank you for your love in this act of forgiveness.

GOD, I simply forgive.

CHAPTER 17

LIFE AFTER ABUSE

WHEN I WAS a little girl, my father had sent me from America a red umbrella with beautiful abstract white images woven into, and I could not wait to carry it gracefully over my head to church that Sunday. Mummy warned me that the umbrella was fragile and I needed to be careful because it was going to rain that day. And rain it did. That Sunday the showers were heavy, the wind was gusting mightily, and I struggled to protect my umbrella. Sadly, the raging winds ripped it apart before I could even close it. I remember standing in the pouring rain bawling my eyes out. My precious umbrella was gone and there was no patching it back together. No matter how beautiful my umbrella, it was not design to withstand the raging wind.

Sometimes our lives can feel like that. Some tragic event happens and we feel helpless. An unexpected train wreck. We stand there looking at the ruined places, wondering how we can recover from this disaster. Childhood trauma is like that. It just happens. One day you are playing with a friend and out of nowhere, some unusual thing happens. You are touched, kissed, groped, or pinned down unexpectedly. It's sudden. It's aggressive. It's manipulative. It's seductive. It leaves us shocked and confused. Before we can wrap our heads around it, something precious is ripped away by the furious culprit of violence, coercion, and manipulation. From that moment nothing is the same. We are left broken, ashamed, and afraid.

When one is abused, especially for a long period of time, it becomes difficult to get life back on track. Every attempt at wholeness seems pointless. The missing years of our childhood, the stolen months without joy and countless hours trying to come up from the pit, make recovery quite a difficult task to conquer.

But God is capable of redeeming *all* broken things. He never runs out of solutions. There are no limits, no boundaries, and no extent to which God won't go for us. We are all worthy of rescue. God might not give you a wedding story, like he gave me, but He will give you a testimony of Himself if we allow Him to narrate our journey. It will take us partaking in His goodness by believing, *"All things are working together for our good."* The Spirit of God is a regenerator. It enables us to be renewed. In Lamentations 3:22–23 it says, *"Because of the Lord's great love we are not consumed, for his compassion never fails. His mercies are new every morning."* Every day when our eyes are open to see daylight, we can start a new chapter. There is hope. We have access to a new life. New opportunities. We have a future. We do no not have to live a life of torment and despair. Abiding in this spiritual truth takes us from devastation to liberation, from disappointment to encouragement.

I know you are probably thinking, "Easier said than done, Jozanne." I totally understand. It took me eight years to get to a place where I can say healing has taken place. Sexual assault is one of the worst violations anyone can experience. Sexual violence has taken many lives, spiritually, and unfortunately, physically. *"On average, there are 321,500 victims (age 12 or older) of rape and sexual assault each year in the United States."* (RAINN) That means every ninety-eight seconds a human being experiences one of the most horrifying crimes against their soul, especially children.

When a child is born, they are born with an innate hopefulness, an innate faith that everything will work out fine. Just take a look at children and watch the excitement in their eyes, the optimism. Even when you offend them, they are so willing to forgive. This child has hope and their little spirit is full of life.

When children are sexually violated, it damages their soul. The constant destruction to a child's soul will eventually turn into despair. It leaves scars on the soul, like rejection, abandonment, fear, violence, mistrust, inferiority, insecurity, and the like. Because these scars are difficult to escape, they usually end up controlling us. We fall prey to helplessness and hopelessness because we believe there is no eternal cure for this spiritual death of the inner man.

Sometimes rape is far worse than murder. At least when we die physically, we go and get to be with God, but with rape, the wounded soul feels like it is continually being murdered. For centuries, society has tried to come to terms with how to cure someone whose soul has been murdered. The best we as a society can come up with are coping methods. It's wonderful to cope, but it is marvelous to be free and renewed. In scripture, we are told that there is a final destination for everyone that has been scarred by life's woes. It is called death to the old man. For the believer, *"Anyone who is baptized into Christ, Jesus is baptized into his death."* We are convinced that as long as the One died, all died. What does that mean? It is the revelation of the cross.

By faith that creature is put to death through the spiritual cross. Just as Jesus died to the flesh and was risen by the spirit, we too are capable of spiritual regeneration. The scars that used to control us are all put to death. These scars can no longer use us like strings on a marionette to make our lives miserable. We no longer dwell in a damaged place. We become born of a different spirit. No longer do we make decisions from a place of insecurity and fear. The strings are cut and we are free. From the beginning of time God had a plan for mankind that would restore us to our rightful place after spiritual death. It's demonstrated through the cross.

The revelation behind the cross is not some silly, made up story. For those who believe, it is the perfect remedy for man's brokenness and separation from the love of God. Understanding the cross allows us to see with spiritual eyes that God holds all things together. The exhibition of the cross is the expression of God's heart. In it he expresses His pure love of sacrifice, dedication, and affirmation.

The love of God displayed enables us to resolve that our old life no longer needs to define us. We can give our old self a funeral, say a eulogy, and cover the grave. We are no longer subjected to the past or its secrets.

Since touring with my solo play, *Beautiful*, I have encountered hundreds of people who have kept their secret for decades. Take for instance the woman in Georgia I mentioned earlier. She did not have the courage to tell her mother about her rape until she was fifty years old. By that time, her perpetrator had died. For over *four decades* she held in this secret. *"I weighed 285 pounds when I told my mother the truth,"* she said. *"Shortly after that, I dropped 89 pounds in four months."* Wow! How many of us are still backpacking other people's junk spiritually due to keeping it a secret? This woman was afraid and ashamed to share the secret with her mother because her perpetrator was a dear friend of the family. She did not want to disappoint or upset her mother.

Another woman in her sixties stood up at a woman's conference after she saw an excerpt from *Beautiful* and shared how her college professor had kissed her on the cheek in a very inappropriate manner after luring her into his office to go over her thesis. She stated that although he never kissed her lips or did anything else, she carried this shame for many years. As I watched her speak about the situation, I could see her getting choked up. *"I never wanted anyone to think I was a whore,"* she said. *"He was my mother's friend and I did not want to disappoint her. I was so ashamed that if anyone found out, people would think different of me."*

Her shame was about the helplessness she felt in that office with a professor she once respected. She was ashamed for not standing up for herself and for keeping it a secret for such a long time. For over forty years she tried to hold on to her dignity and regain control of her life. Nevertheless, when she shared this secret for the first time among a group of people where she felt safe, her tears testified of her freedom. She finally gave herself permission to be heard. She had found her voice beneath the silence.

Victims of abuse carry these secrets because they feel somehow they played a role in this vicious act of violence. We feel guilty. I can't tell you how many times I have blamed myself for the abuse I encountered as a child. Victims of abuse need answers, and when there are no solutions, more than likely we give ourselves an answer just to make peace with the spiritual death we feel.

According to RAINN, *"As of 1998, 17.7 million American women have been victims of attempted or completed rape, as well as 2.78 million men."* This could be any female taking a walk or innocently visiting a trusted friend. When we hear the word "rape" we envision some woman walking down the street and getting grabbed by a complete stranger, yet innocent people are violated daily simply by doing ordinary things. The deed is done and the future seems impossible. We ask ourselves what life will be like after abuse. We are not certain we will be able to function. We battle with our thoughts daily and feel despondent when they just don't go away. I am a witness. Here is the good news. There is life after abuse. We do not need to handle it alone. God has placed people just like He has planted trees to refresh, revitalize, and provide spiritual healing that nourishes us back to life.

A few years ago I went with my friend Brittany on a getaway to the Grand Canyon. Early one morning around 6am I sat on the balcony to meditate. A huge, majestic Freemont Cottonwood tree stood a few feet away from our balcony at the edge of the woods. We rarely acknowledge their presence. We forget how vital trees are for our living; we forget they have purpose. They not only decorate the Earth's landscape, but without them we would die.

They represent life by providing us oxygen. Trees are responsible for cooling the city streets when there is excessive heat, they help prevent water pollution by breaking rainfall, thus allowing the water to flow down the trunk and into the earth below the tree. They are the foundation of our food chain, and play a vital role in ecology— purifying the air of carbon dioxide. Basically, trees are essential to our survival.

I believe just as God provided trees because he knew we would live in a polluted world, He in His great wisdom created Spirit filled individuals to refresh us when life is ablaze. These are the individuals that speak life into our dead situations, ensuring we do not remain contaminated by the spiritual pollution that comes with life's tragedy. If you look around, you can see life givers around you, and if you don't see them, go on a mission to find them.

We have a Good Shepherd that has gone before us to make the crooked path straight, ensuring we don't remain victims or make excuses for never rising to our full potential. We must resolve who we will become in this life. To obtain our freedom, we must fight for it. God has declared through His word, that *"wherever the Spirit of the Lord is, there is freedom."* We must understand that God already gave us freedom and it is our birthright. It belongs to us. Yes, YOU. Freedom belongs to you. We don't have to beg for it, we just need to grab hold of it. However, if we don't believe we already have freedom, it will be difficult to pursue it.

Imagine a homeless person who is destitute and hungry, sitting on the side of the street. A stranger passes by and immediately their heart is filled with compassion. They have a beautiful home, filled with every kind of food and delicacies. Their home is warm and cozy. Everything this homeless person needs abides in this house. They will lack nothing. This stranger bends down, hands them the keys and whispers, "This is your key to your new home."

Instead of jumping for joy and gratitude, the homeless person looks at the stranger as if this was a joke and laughs in their face. It's useless trying to convince them because they don't believe. Even when the stranger leaves the key in their hands, the homeless person looks at the key with mere amusement and remains in his situation. I believe at times we all have done that. The keys to freedom are given to us through the power of the Holy Spirit but we doubt. The Spirit of God visits all of us. We feel the pull, we get close, we dine with Him, but we never taste and see that He is good. Although the key is in our hands, we never enter through the door. *"You study the Scriptures diligently because you think that in them you have eternal life. Yet you refuse to come to me to have life."* John 5:40–41. Just like the homeless man, we remain stuck in our situation when freedom is our inheritance.

Girl, go get your freedom. It belongs to you. There are treasures locked in our father's house waiting for us to grab hold of. Our breakthrough is at our fingertips but unbelief prevents us from taking a hold of it. May we continue to pray for our faith to increase. This is the time to go beyond brave. Take a bold step of faith and recover the life God intended for you and who He has called you to be.

Maybe you have lost friends and family in the process of speaking the truth. The loneliness creeps in and you think it was better being surrounded by those who abused you rather than being alone. I have found myself there many times. At the age of eighteen, I could care less that an ex-boyfriend was beating and cheating on me. As long as I was not alone, it felt comfortable living with the lie. It did not matter that my heart was shattered and there was a possibility of me losing a limb or my life. I refused to let anyone know he did not love me. I was ashamed, and I was afraid. Afraid to leave the only guy that helped me after I ran away from home, yet he was also the only guy who punched me in my ribs, beat me with a belt, and left me to walk home eighteen blocks in the pouring rain at 1 am in the morning.

Living an abundant life after abuse can seem like a long haul but it is worth investing in your healing. For those of us abused by a stranger or a friend, our road to recovery becomes a place where we have to learn to trust again, feel safe again, and be free again. For those who have been abused by a family member, it has brought on so many other dysfunctions. We often go into isolation, losing the precious gift of family. We become lone rangers, and have to learn how to show up on our own.

We must not confuse relatives for family. Family does not have to be biological. It is any group of people who nurture, value, and protect us in the development of becoming a whole human being. Most of my "family" is from different races and backgrounds. There were times when the homeless community showed me more love and affection than my own family, I'm sad to say. That is why Jesus said, *"Who is my father and mother? Only those who do the will of God."* And what is the will of God? It is to love God with all our heart, soul, and mind. It is to love our neighbor as ourselves.

Many parents are great in accomplishing the goal of raising children. Then there are some of us who were abused, abandoned, and rejected by our biological parents. They teach us fear instead of love. These abusive relationships leave us to handle life on our own if no one steps in to truly take care of us. Some people spend their entire life fruitlessly trying to find Daddy or Mommy in other people, which can leave us asking, "How am I able to move on with life?"

How do we find solace after our relatives abandons us? We find peace that our birth didn't begin with our parents; it began with an intentional God. He allowed us to be born and He has an amazing plan for our lives despite our flaws. There is a bigger picture as to why we were born. It is difficult to make sense of the chaos, but in it God is willing to sign His signature and leave His handprint. We must trust that God has a plan no matter what our lives look like.

Like every human being, our parents are accountable for the role they are given and we are not liable for their mistakes. The only thing we are responsible for is getting past the offense. At some point we are responsible for our own healing. We are accountable for owning our faith in God and coming into agreement with Him about who *He* says we are. We must not fall into the trap of self-pity, but focus on how God can get glory out of our lives. Of course, God is not insensitive to our woes, He empathizes with every pain we experience, but

He does not want us to remain there. He wants us to rise up and press to the mark of a higher calling. There is a purpose for every human being in this world. God gives man an allotted time to accomplish a great task that will benefit mankind, and sometimes in the midst of that assignment we encounter tragedy.

This reminds me of Joshua when his mentor, Moses, died. Joshua was devastated. The person who taught him all he knew, treated him like a son, and gave him perspective on life was in the grave. Scripture shows us, *"The Israelites grieved for Moses in the plains of Moab thirty days, until the time of weeping and mourning was over."* Deuteronomy 34:8. Notice it says, *"...until the time mourning was over."* There is a time for everything under the sun. *"There is a time to mourn and a time to dance,"* Ecclesiastes 3:4, and when the mourning was over, God told Joshua, *"I will be with you; I will never leave you nor forsake you. Be strong and courageous, because you will lead these people to inherit the land I swore to their ancestors to give them."* Joshua 1:5–6. God had a plan for Joshua and the people of Israel. He wanted them to move on and accomplish His will on Earth. God had spoken a word for the children of Israel to get to the Promised Land and Joshua had the baton to finish the race. It was up to Joshua to not dwell on the pain of the past or the fear of the future in order to fulfill the calling on His life.

Beloved, God spoke a word over your life and it will take faith to carry it out despite the adversity. Our identity is never defined by misfortune. As a matter a fact, identity gets revealed through catastrophe. *"Now if we are children, then we are heirs—heirs of God and co-heirs with Christ, if indeed we share in his sufferings in order that we may also share in his glory. I consider that our present sufferings are not worth comparing with the glory that will be revealed in us. For the creation waits in eager expectation for the children of God to be revealed. For the creation was subjected to frustration, not by its own choice, but by the will of the one who subjected it, in hope that the creation itself will be liberated from its bondage to decay and brought into the freedom and glory of the children of God."* Romans 8:17–21. Great adversity creates the urgency to discover the truth and we not only get a glimpse of God, we recognize our true selves.

Maybe you believe *"I will never be anything"* or *"I am ugly."* You have been abused, and you rehearse abusive thoughts about yourself in your mind. Beautiful, it's time to get your confidence back. It's time to get your life back.

Loving ourselves takes work. It will take us unlearning the lies of the past. It will take us digging into God's Word. It will take spending time alone. It will take us being bold enough to walk away and let go of old relationships and old habits that have us stagnant. Don't think for one minute this is an overnight miracle. It will take time! Remember, God works with fruit. For a seed to manifest into something delicious, it goes through a process that takes a substantial amount of time. We have to plant God's word in our hearts, water it every day, and let Him do marvelous things through it. It is important not to rush the process by trying to grow our fruit with artificial fertilizers. We will have quick fruit, and those around us will soon realize that we have no true substance.

I love the fact that God takes his time, because anything that has an ounce of worth is never an overnight success. There must be labor and toiling to fully have wisdom and understanding.

Even my mother, Jean pursued her healing behind those walls of the hospital. She too came full circle. She got up every day, contributed to the people around her, prayed, shared her story, and even came to the point where she wanted to take care of a child. Her pain and shame in the past made her throw away her child, but God's grace, love and healing gave her an opportunity before she died to nurture and love a baby who was beaten and throw away by her own mother.

Time and faith is a prerequisite for recovery when it comes to abuse or any catastrophe. Do we believe we are worth starting over? Do we think we are worth loving? Do we believe we are worth the rescue? Beneath all the pain and shame, do we still believe we have value? It is the defining moment in our lives. Like I shared, mine was at the age of twenty-three. I had to make a decision that everything that happened to me prior to that moment would propel me to victory and not plunge me into defeat. We must *choose* to come in *agreement* with God on identity. Our past is not our story. It's merely the beginning. Remember, everything in God is finished. We are just experiencing life through time.

There is life after abuse. There is love after divorce. There is promise after the loss of a child. There is always hope after every tragedy. If you are still breathing, God is not finished with you yet. *"Blessed are those who mourn, for they will be comforted."* Matthew 5:4. Our loving Father is watching over His words to perform it in our lives. He wants to come in and dine with us. Just like Joshua, God wants us to move forward. We have wept and wallowed in despair far too long. Let it go. Grieve no more. God gave Joshua thirty days. Sometimes we are still grieving years, even decades later. There is a time for everything in life. A time of mourning and a time of rejoicing. Your Heavenly Father wants you to find hope again. He desires to rekindle the fire of purpose in our lives again.

I know emotional pain is difficult to get through, but we must not heed the voice that tells us we will not survive. We will not perish. Be strong and courageous, beautiful one, and let's go! You can do it. God is with you. *"The joy of the Lord is your strength."* May He be your shield and buckler, may you trust the works of His hands, and may your heart leap for joy when you think of the journey ahead. There is life after abuse. Go get it. Leave the past behind and win your race.

You are worth it.

CHAPTER 18

KNIGHTS AND PRINCESSES

A BAG OF kettle popcorn, a firm pillow, and bottle of kombucha is all I need for a romantic movie on a Friday night. And don't forget the box of tissue close at hand for when Cinderella's shoes fit, and Rose in *Titanic* runs through a deluge of water to find her Jack. Oh, and how can we forget Allison and Noah in *The Notebook*? Love stories. We all love them and desire to encounter them. There is always a knight and a princess in our heads. We all desire to be the object of someone's affection.

"The best love is the kind that awakens the soul and makes us reach for more. It plants a fire in our hearts and brings peace to our mind, and that's what you have given me." This is one of my favorite lines from *The Notebook*, written by Nicholas Sparks. As Allie reads these powerful words in a letter from her long lost love, the audience could not help but shed tears because we all long for this kind of eternal love. It's a love we cannot do without. It fuels our drive to live and it's unforgettable.

From the innocence of pigtails to the iniquity of one night stands, the desire to love another human being with all of our being and have that same love reciprocated is a constant desire. We crave it, and sometimes we even fear it. It's vulnerable, powerful, and reveals us. Tell me, which girl did not want the prince to kiss Snow White or for Beauty to love the Beast? We make every effort to fight for love whether in the movies, on our favorite TV shows, or cartoons. Love must win. The majority of little girls fantasize about being swept off their feet by a handsome prince, spirited away to an exotic palace, and being treated like a princess.

As adults, our imagination runs wild on our first date. Wedding dresses are already picked out and the honeymoon planned before our dream date takes the first bite out of his food. *Pick me. Chose me. Cherish me. Care for me.* This is not a woman thing; men are included as well. Most men desire a woman with exquisite qualities and the perfect measurements. But I assure you, after he wraps his arms around her bottle-shaped figure, he must feel the warmth of her heart. Have you ever wondered why people desire this kind of love? Could it be that our creator is sending a message to our hearts from the throne room of Heaven?

Is it possible that, *"Eternity is in the hearts of man but he cannot fathom it?"* Ecclesiastes 3:11. Could it be possible that the idea of the perfect man and the beautiful woman, who lives happily after in a castle far away started with God? Has anyone really wondered why people are fascinated by this kind of redemptive love story? Could it be possible that such an affair of the heart does exist? And if it does exist, where and with whom do we find this kind of passion and relentless affection? Truthfully, the only kind of love I have heard of with reckless abandon is the story of the cross. It is the greatest story ever told to mankind of an invisible God that expressed His love from eternity by making Jesus a tangible language of love. It is not blind faith without substance. We are able to touch it, see it, and hear about it. It came with action and power. It was not secretive and complicated. This love had depth, intention, and demonstrated its willingness to go to any lengths for me.

"For God so loved the world He sent forth His only begotten son, that whosoever believes in Him should not perish, but have eternal life." John 3:16. According to Christian Headlines, *"Denver Broncos quarterback Tim Tebow passed for 316 yards in a playoff win—leading to John 3:16*

becoming the most searched item on Google." Whether you are a believer or not, we can safely say that the majority of Americans know this verse. We have seen it on bumper stickers, cups, greeting cards, and bookmarks. But what exactly does it mean? Who said these words? If we search scripture, we will discover that Jesus said these words himself. And what I find most fascinating is that he was not preaching in the temple, but speaking to one person: Nicodemus, a Pharisee who followed the law religiously and was very influential within Judaism.

Nicodemus secretly met with Jesus at night to learn the secret things of the spiritual kingdom. After much discussion about what it means to be born again, Jesus shared later in the chapter, *"For God so loved the world He sent forth His only begotten son, that whosoever believes in Him should not perish, but have eternal life."* Why was it so important for Jesus to disclose this information to such a man? One, Nicodemus being a Pharisee, saw himself as righteous without really taking a look at the state of his heart. Jesus wanted Nicodemus to know that his religious works were not the prerequisite for being a son of God. He wanted Nicodemus to know that without receiving the love of God and having that impartation spiritually, Nicodemus was far off and incapable of loving others the way God did. Another fascinating thing was the intimacy between Jesus and Nicodemus. Love is intimate, not in a sexual way, but in a more similar way to a heart to heart conversation between two people.

Jesus needed Nicodemus to know the main reason for such an epic event was because of love. God had his eyes on mankind way before the foundation of the world and it was the object of His affection. Through the ugliness and despair in the world, God saw the depth of mankind's beauty. It intrigued Him; He was willing to give anything for it, even His only son, Jesus Christ. For the parents who have an only child, would you give up their life for anyone? I doubt it. That child is your heart. I recently had a friend who lost her one and only son and it's the most devastating loss any parent can encounter. What do you think God is saying through the message of the Cross? The heart of the Father is love. And Jesus was the heart of the Father. God is saying through the message of the Cross, "Here is my heart. This is how much I love you." Nothing compares to it. It is the greatest sign to mankind of how zealous God is for every human being.

Now I know we don't always feel like He loves us every day, especially when we encounter trials. Like with a newly married couple, the novelty of courtship and the honeymoon fades, the love is being tested, and we start wondering why we got married in the first place. Nevertheless, regardless of the pain that sometimes comes with love, we all at one point fight for the epic love story.

We all want to be loved, and without it, the meaning of life seems useless. Like a plant needs water to live, a human being needs love to thrive. Love compels us to move forward in its direction and the only thing that will hold us back is the past. Past abuse will make us run from giving or receiving love.

Because of my painful past life experiences, I had become jaded and practical about love. Something inside of me died. For several years it was difficult rediscovering that girl who loved without reservation. The true essence of who I am was buried beneath all the ruined things in my life. I had forgotten that I was a princess, knitted by a King whose affection for me was not just unconditional, but potent enough to transform my life. But when our hearts are broken, it's difficult to spiritually see and hear. Our hearts are so valuable. It is there where treasures lies. It is one of our main physical life forces, but also our emotional life energy. This is why we should guard our hearts.

When we give it away to things, situations, and people undeserving to the value it holds, we ultimately will lose faith in God's goodness and love. There is always a cost to giving our hearts to perishable things. *"For where your treasure is, there your heart will be also."* Matthew 6:21.

Looking more in depth at this scripture, we can see that God connects the heart with treasures. Webster's dictionary defines the word "treasure" as a (1): wealth, stored up or hoarded, buried *treasure*

(2): wealth of any kind or in any form: riches. It is also defined as wealth or riches stored or accumulated. When I reflect on how many times I have given my heart to the wrong person, as well as the things that fade away, it's no wonder why it took me several years to recover from the trauma and devastation of giving away valuable things to unworthy people. Handing over valuable things into the hands of the immature will always leave us broken. Imagine giving a child an expensive diamond ring. What would they do with it? They would probably lose it in the dirt outside in their sandbox. It is clear that God has great investment in the heart for the amount of time He allows it to beat. *"The LORD is good to all: and his tender mercies are over all his works."* Psalms 145:9.

First, let's take a good look at our physical heart. Without it, we are dead. This organ weighs ¾ of a pound and has beat approximately seventy times per minute since the day we were born. That would be 4,200 times an hour, over 100,000 times a day, and over 35 million times a year. I don't know about you but this makes me think about how every heartbeat of my life was used. Really, why is your heart beating right now? Why is the God of the Universe allowing us another second? If we had to place a price on our heartbeats, we would be billionaires.

The word heart is mentioned 925 times in scripture, which leads us to the conclusion that God feels strongly about it. And this is the reason why we must consider what we love and who we love. When we invest in love that's filled with empty promises and rhetoric from people who lack integrity, our hearts will suffer pain every time. *"Above all else, guard your heart, for everything you do flows from it."* Proverbs 4:23. Our hearts are rivers of water and if we are not careful, they can become muddy potholes from all the toxic waste thrown into it.

The heart hungers for romance, excitement, mystery, and glamour. It longs to be chased and wooed. It is the kind of love that is *"patient, kind, does not envy, does not boast, keeps no record of wrong, it trusts all things, believes all things, and it protects."* The quest for true love begins with having a relationship with Love itself. It is in that secret place of divine revelation and spiritual encounter with God that we are removed from the fantasy of romance and thrown into the sea of love.

No one can grant us that kind of love except for God. This is one of the most profound truths and if believed and pursued, it will set us free from the snare of flattery and disappointment when human love fails us. In our lifetime a few people will demonstrate these Godly qualities close to perfectly, but nothing can be compared to the unfailing affection of God. God uses everything in our lives to show his glorious face and to draw us to His perfect love.

God cries for our hearts each day. He wants an intimate relationship with us. He longs for our affection not because He necessarily needs it, but so he can have fellowship and reveal more of Himself in us. But when our hearts are broken, it's difficult to have communion with anyone. We become a stranger to kindness, gentleness, and love.

I had left some valuable treasures in the hands of one-night stands, abusive boyfriends, and my own father. My knights turned into villains, and my heart was fractured by all the broken relationships I had encountered. The freedom to walk in my femininity and not despise its beauty became a challenge. Being a woman and being wooed by her king no longer was a desire. I became callous, aggressive, and cold to love. To believe God loved me was too lofty for my mind to conceive. My faith in love had drowned in a sea of doubt far too long and the possibility of rescue seemed impossible.

I desperately needed a love encounter with God before I could open the door of my heart again. I was looking for God through things, people, and situations, not realizing that *"the only thing that counts is faith expressing itself through love."* Galatians 5:6. This love relationship between God and me could be trusted, but it would take practice. It would take encountering his goodness countless times through stepping out on faith every time I answered the call. Every time God calls us to step out on faith and we take it, it's an opportunity to gain trust again and experience divine love. Love lives in the realm of the supernatural.

It goes beyond ourselves and in order to give love, we have to receive it first. And to receive love, it takes a place of solitude to be with the Author of love—God. It takes knowing and loving ourselves in God. This time of solitude will remind us why the night air smells like heaven, the sun burns passionately, why we were created, and most importantly, for getting familiar again with the sweet sound of God's voice. It's in this place God reveals that his love is trustworthy. He reveals His nature and definition of love and that we are not only able to give it to others but also able to recognize it when it is in front of us. God's love is not careless but has a reckless abandon that burns like a fire.

And what do I mean by that? God in his character is not careless where He does not think through consequences. He is reckless with compassion and passion that he is willing to abandon everything just for you. He will leave the ninety-nine sheep and go for the one. And once we encounter this reckless abandon, it transforms us. It ignites our hearts on fire that we have no other choice but to respond with the same recklessness. Kind of like when Rose in *Titanic* was roaming through the waters for Jack. She loved him and would not leave that ship until she found him. Rose and Jack had found love and they would do anything to keep it.

This reckless love is an action of faith in a God we can rely on to protect our hearts. It's the kind of recklessness that makes us desperate for change and is sometimes illogical. Like the day the Spirit of God led me to not use my credit cards anymore and trust Him that He was going to provide my rent and car payment. At the time, I needed 736 dollars total to pay my bills. Without a penny to my name, I surrendered my faith and forbid myself to use my credit card or to borrow any money from friends. A few weeks later I was invited to a conference by a friend. Once there, the speaker recognized me from an event where I had performed spoken word. He asked me to come up and perform that same poem.

After my performance, he told those in attendance to make a donation if they were blessed by my poetry. There were only fifty people in the room that night and not everyone gave, yet that night I walked away with 750 dollars cash. It was exactly what I needed to pay my bills. Can somebody say Praise God! God once again was showing me that He is faithful. He was showing me that he cared about my needs. He was showing me that I was loved not just by others, but from Heaven. He was showing me that everything that concerned me meant the world to Him.

As someone who came from an abusive past, it was extremely difficult for me to trust God's character and accept that He loved *all* of me. But the truth is God is always ready to lavish His love over us without any reservation. It's through His eyes we see our wholeness. Through His eyes we are flawless. This is where a love encounter begins. *"For I know the plans I have for you,' declares the Lord. 'One to prosper you and not to harm you. Plans to give you a hope and a future.'"* Jeremiah 29:11.

A true love encounter with God will not only transform us, it will take some dying to the past. Just like Jesus, his death seemed final, but that was not the end of the story. When they went to the tomb to find him, it was empty. We also must die to our past and experience the resurrection power of the Holy Spirit. This way, when people show up and touch the wounded places, we are no longer living there. Those grave clothes have been removed and the old man no longer abides there. We no longer respond to life through our brokenness.

The word of God says *"anyone in Christ is a new creation, the old is gone and the new has come."* From that moment onwards we can have that same hope and childlike faith like when we were younger. Scripture says *"unless you become like one of these little children, you cannot enter the kingdom of Heaven."* Do you want childlike faith? Do you want to be made new again? It is possible!

Creation itself stands testimony to His divine attributes and His invisible nature, and we see the most beautiful analogy of this in God's creation. We see the lowly caterpillar, destined to crawl its life upon a tree, a very limited lifestyle. This creature's only option is to use its little legs to crawl. All its life, no one helps it. It is at the mercy of the environment. Before we had a love encounter with the Heavenly father, we were just like the caterpillar.

The pain of our past creates loneliness and sadness when no one is around. Material things become meaningless, and we still feel an empty void. Eventually, if we are not healed from the inside out, we too become prey just like the caterpillar to our environment.

But one day the caterpillar will case itself in his own tomb and it will die. It does not change, it dies, and its very molecular structure is broken down to a subatomic soup. It's gone. Dead. From the outside, it looks like a miserable life. Death is final. But unseen to outside eyes, within the cocoon, a divine miracle begins to take place. Another DNA begins to take form, completely unlike the creature before.

One day the tomb breaks open wide and out flies one of nature's most beautiful creatures, a butterfly. No longer bound by its environment, it soars beyond the skies to a far off place which was inconceivable before. It is difficult to catch. It will soar, and people admire its beauty. They forget that at one point this creature was just slime. It's free and it's beautiful.

When we look upon this creature we see God's delicate will. We see its delicate frame, unhindered. It's one of God's ways to show us that He can change anyone. Just like the caterpillar, we break out of our own cocoon in our rebirth and sail on the winds of God's will.

No longer will we strive for love and affection from any other source. No longer will we live in regret, pain, and anger from what others have done to us. God's love becomes our thermal current. Now we sail on His wings and have life and life more abundantly. This is the revelation of the resurrection life of Jesus Christ. This is the greatest love encounter and nothing in this world or the world unseen to our naked eyes will separate us from the love of Christ. He is the prince in shining armor and we are the Beloved of God! Our past is forgotten and all the world sees is the miraculous beauty of a new you.

LOVE

Love will come outside and kiss you in the rain
Love risks everything to have you.
You are the object of its affection
Love lays down its life.
Love tells the truth
Love is endless
Love is wrapped in a one-word definition.
GOD

Our identity is much bigger than our abuse. The love God has for us is powerful enough to wash away our sufferings. *"I know the heart knows its own bitterness."* Proverbs 14:10. And because no one has walked in our shoes, they will not understand the depth of our loss.

Jesus knows the severity of our suffering. Not only does He know it, He shares in it through the cross. He has demonstrated His love in perfection that we might put our faith in something substantial again. The scripture says, *"He was despised and rejected by men; a man of sorrows, and acquainted with grief."* Isaiah 53:3. Jesus is acquainted with grief more than any person in the world. Just imagine, a man without sin who served and loved everyone was abused by hateful words, rejected, and beaten beyond recognition. I am sure He can relate to the injustice we feel. He empathizes with the deepness of our affliction and sorrow. That is why He is our High Priest and intercessor.

He knows more than anyone else how to be victorious over grief. God does see all the wickedness and injustices that take place. *"He is well acquainted with your grief, and he will never leave you."* John 14:18.

When we allow ourselves to have a love encounter with our Knight in shining armor, we will see that He has the last word of our future. The abuse we suffered is not the most significant part of your story.

KNIGHTS AND PRINCESSES

One of my favorite stories in the Bible is about Joseph. He was abused and betrayed by his family. He was thrown in a pit and left for dead by his own brothers. He encountered problems on every side. A free man once loved by his father was now a slave in a strange land. Joseph was falsely accused and spent unnecessary years behind bars. But God had a plan. Jesus was the author and perfector of His faith and ultimately had the last words about His life.

Despite the horrible things Joseph suffered, we see further down in scripture that God eventually changed Joseph's circumstances. Yet it was more than merely that; God used those trials to circumcise Joseph's heart. Joseph came face to face with those who betrayed him, and he had two choices. He could be vengeful and bitter, or be the person God called him to be, redeemed, filled with God's love and mercy. He did not allow his past to dictate the outcome of his identity. He said to his brothers, *"As for you, you meant evil against me, but God meant it for good, to bring it about that many people should be kept alive, as they are today."*

Beautiful one, your pain is not the end product of who you are. God is at work in you just like He was in Joseph. Abuse is not the final destination to your life. There is a greater purpose beyond our abuse. Everything that happens in our lives is to take us back to the face of our creator. Beloved, how we enter the world is not under our control but how we exit is our choice. Paul said, *"But one thing I do, forgetting those things which are behind and reaching forward to those things which are ahead. I press toward the goal for the prize of the upward call of God in Christ Jesus."* Philippians 3:12.

Paul decided to not only press forward, but to *look upward.* Our desire for knights and princesses is there in our hearts for a reason because such a love affair does exist. It is a void placed there to tug on our hearts that we can pursue and reconnect with the truth that God is love. And His love never fails.

Love always wins.

CHAPTER 19

A VERTICAL LEAP

THERE ARE TIMES when God allows our paths to cross with people whose lives are so infectious it gives us the permission to live life with audacity. A friend of mine, Lisa Nicole, invited me to her birthday parties for the weekend. Yes, *parties*. She had the audacity to have three separate events to celebrate life with her friends. Impressed by the appreciation she had for life, that morning as we left the Bleu Café on Melrose, for the first time I was inspired to celebrate my birthday.

Of all the things I could do for my birthday, I decided to participate in trapeze flying at the Santa Monica Pier. It always intrigued me to see the daredevils flying high. At the same time I couldn't help but think about the hundreds of things that could possibly go wrong once I was flying in the air. I might die. I might miss the safety net and hit the ground. I might be thrown to the boardwalk and everyone would laugh at me. Despite all the negative thoughts, I signed up and was ready to go.

There was no turning back since I invited my two best friends to come and watch. The instructor explained it was going to take four simple steps. Climb the ladder, let go of the bar behind me, jump off the board, and enjoy the ride. It sounds so simple until you get twenty-three feet in the air and think to yourself, *"WHAT IN THE WORLD WERE YOU THINKING!"*

A VERTICAL LEAP

"All I want you to do, Jozanne, is let go of the bar behind you and hold the swing in front of you," the instructor reiterated. "Let go, Jozanne. She held onto the belt strapped around my waist. "JUMP!" I knew I had to let go of the bar at some point, but I was holding on for dear life, even though the instructor assured me countless times of my safety and I saw the huge net below.

With my entire body shaking and adrenaline pumping, I took a huge leap off the board, swinging in the air, screaming to the hearing of everyone on the pier. The fear. The trauma of being thrown into the unknown can definitely be terrifying.

I did not understand why I was so overwhelmed. But there was only one way down and that was to let go of the swing. Finally, it dawned on me that I was not afraid of heights, but I was afraid of letting go.

My hands burned from the friction on the rope and my forearm lost its ability to hold me up any longer. Down I went, landing safely on the net. Every cell in my body felt alive. I was conscious of my breath, my shaky legs, and the adrenaline running through my body. I laid there for a moment and realized how alive I felt, but also how scared I was. I was scared and extremely emotional. I knew in my heart that God had a message in my jumping and I needed to receive it.

On the ground, my friend Andrea had tears in her eyes. There was definitely something spiritual about jumping. I decided to climb the ladder again, just as nervous as the first time. I wanted to get to the root of what had me so shaken up. After my fifth jump it came to me that I was not only afraid of letting go, but I was also fearful of not being caught. Because most of my life I was dropped by the people I trusted the most, a simple task like letting go of the trapeze was difficult. You would think after all these years working on my emotional health, I would be completely over it. But the truth is that there is no absolute final destination to healing. There is always room for growth. No matter how young or old we are, we can always evolve and become better than we were.

Many of us are still carrying childhood wounds that are preventing us from jumping into our destiny. Whenever we want change we must take vertical leaps. The trapeze was built strong and safe enough to carry me, but it was going to take me pressing past my inner fears to experience a ride of a lifetime. Because of various issues in our lives we tend to doubt God's integrity to catch us when we take a leap of faith. But faith is faith no matter how big or small it appears. Faith will always be rewarded. This is why the scripture says *"If you have faith as small as a mustard seed, it will move mountains."* Matthew 17:20. I am convinced that there is one sin and it is unbelief. Unbelief can lead us to make irrational decisions that will ultimately delay the promise or destroy our destiny.

Sometimes we have to make up in our minds that we will let go of the excuses and fully believe God's word about who He says we are. And that is what I did. That Sunday evening after leaving the pier, I repented for running away from giants when God had given me everything in my hand to be a giant slayer. It's never easy bouncing back from pain. But if we put our faith in God, by taking the first step up the ladder with our broken past, letting go of all we know to be true and jump into grace, we will land on a miracle.

Scripture says, *"Faith is the substance of things hoped for and the evidence of things not seen."* Hebrews 11:1. What are you hoping for? Is it peace? Is it love? Is it healing? Is it freedom? We must remember, faith is a substance, which means it is something concrete. It is tangible. It has weight. It is not something that is abstract. That which we hope for has evidence, even though we cannot see it with the naked eye. Another word for evidence is "sign" or "testimony." Whenever we operate in faith there will be a testimony because there is substance behind it. I need to emphasize this because faith is not presumption or a senseless act. To step out on faith comes with what you have heard the Spirit of God whisper in your soul. It is an inner knowing that is not seen with the physical eyes. Some might call it instinct or intuition. It is a conversation between you and Heaven. It is a calling, a request from God to operate in a particular way that expresses His glory in the Earthly realm. Our faith never blesses us alone; it will always bless, inspire, and transform others to interact with Heaven as well. Faith is a supernatural currency that brings us into the abundant life.

Anything we hear God say in the secret place of our heart and we have faith for will manifest into something tangible others can see. A new life demands leaps of faith. We do not visibly see Him but His works display that He exists. Whatever is currently happening in your life that seems overwhelming only needs two things—a word from God and a leap of faith. Faith is the currency of Heaven. We all have a love language. God's love language is always faith. For *"Without faith it is impossible to please God."* Hebrew 11:6.

When a man makes up in his mind that he wants a new life, all it takes is the faith to carry it out. *"Whatever a man thinks so is he."* Proverbs 23:7. There is a false belief that God is unapproachable. We believe that if God wants something He will do it alone. God does nothing alone. He uses man by His Spirit to fulfill His plans in the Earthly realm. He created man with intelligence, a soul, and a conscience in His own image He gives man the wisdom and inspiration to have dominion over the Earth. We are responsible for bringing what is invisible to the realm of the visible.

"The Most High does not live in houses made by human hands." Acts 7:48. We are the Temple of God's Spirit, and His Spirit gives us the power to overcome every affliction. God speaks to us by the Spirit and to our spirit. When He speaks, if we have ears to hear, the one thing He demands is faith. He does not require a theological degree; he does not require us to know every scripture; He does not require us being in church every Sunday. He does not require any works other than faith.

We cannot desire a new experience with God without doing anything different, a new you will require new adjustments. It takes vertical leaps to experience Heaven.

The day I grabbed hold of the truth that the One who created me loved me beyond my understanding, I was transformed. I decided to no longer live my life from my experiences but from the perspective of truth. We don't have to be that girl who just takes what life throws at us. We don't have to sell ourselves short because everything about us is made in God's splendor. We no longer have to live from the place of defeat, but the place of victory. We don't have to operate from a place of brokenness. Let the truth take root in our soul. Give the old you a funeral. Be ready to jump every time life calls for it. Get up from that shameful place and jump. Jump into a relationship with God. Jump into new friendships. Jump on new career paths. Jump out of old habits. Jump into joy. Jump from brokenness to wholeness. Live a life of continuous leaping. When we jump that's when the miracle takes place.

The bravest thing I have ever done was to live. It takes courage to live an authentic life when our circumstances deem us as regular and show us there is nothing to live for. I am not just talking about living as in the sense of breathing and going about the day, but living the life God intended despite the detours. No matter who we are, what race or gender, life happens to us all. It is how we deal with it that will prove what we are made of.

We all have experienced dark situations that have been a thorn in our flesh. Every now and then it reminds us that life is not perfect. It's like dressing up in a beautiful gown and when you look in the mirror, you remember that you lost your arm. Many will put the dress down and not show up at the ball because all they can see is the missing arm, but we forget that all others will see is someone bold enough to show up despite that.

I have learned that, regardless of the heartbreaks, trials, and tribulations I face, all I have to do is show up in life. Show up with what I have. Show up with all my imperfections, unashamed and unafraid. It is very difficult to take vertical leaps with burdens like shame, fear, unforgiveness, bitterness, anger, discouragement, and baggage from our past.

This is the reason I decided to write this book. It is not just to share my journey and story but to remind YOU that you are unique and born for God's glory. A new you *is* possible despite what happened to you.

From when I was a child, I was on a journey to discover who I was and who God is. I needed to know why God took the time to knit me in my mother's womb. Why was I born into poverty and shame? Why was I different from most of the other little children in my neighborhood?

Freedom was a deep desire that kept ringing a bell at the door of my soul. It is the kind of freedom to be who I am at the core of my existence, without any apologies. When someone tells me they want freedom, I believe what they are really saying is, *I just want to be who I was created to be.*

Every situation that occurs in our lives is designed to reveal who we are and why we were born. It is there to challenge our thoughts, awaken our souls, and give us the freedom God planned before the foundation of the world. It is through these adversities the sons of God are manifested. Once again, I am not making a claim that God created these circumstances to teach us a lesson, but if God allows them, God can use them to bring Him glory.

The point of our existence was never to be void of affliction, but to fulfill why we were sent. It is to teach us that we are more than conquerors and that our Spirit is greater than the invisible forces that challenge the Truth that God loves us despite all we have been through.

There is a saying that goes, "God makes no mistakes." I could not agree more. Every human being that has the breath of life in their body is a candidate for a sign and a wonder. When our world is turned topsy-turvy by some tragic event, how do we bounce back? How do we get up after being knocked out? How does one truly become an overcomer?

I am here to tell you good news. Victims can be victors. Get back into the ring of life.

Jesus conquered the grave. This was the sign to the entire universe that with God anything is possible. Jesus showed us the way to victory, that no matter what trials we face in this life, God's power by the Spirit is greater. He did not just leave an autograph; he gave us His name and left us His spirit that we too may overcome.

May we constantly trust in a faithful God that understands our lives and may we walk by faith at the beckoning of His sweet voice. Let truth and love take precedence over our emotions. See the world from God's perspective. Know that lemons can be sour, but they not only make lemonade, they make lemon pies, lemon bars, and lemon soufflé.

One day we will all leave this world behind and enter a world we have not seen. We only get *one* shot here and the question is…Will we allow the past to keep us in a place of bitterness, resentment, anger, and hatred? Let us decide to be unashamed and unafraid of who we are and become who God intended.

"He will not only sustain us, He will deliver our souls from death." Psalms 56:13. God will answer us when we call upon Him. He will be our light and our salvation. There is no need to fear the past having a grip on you. God Himself is our deliverer, our protector, and our Father.

May *this* season of your life be one of great transformation and may the testimony of the King be the final signature to your story. He loves you without reservation. I don't care what wrench was thrown into your life. It does not matter where you were born or what your past has been like, Child of God, you are seen, loved, and heard. Nothing in this world can take your identity unless you allow it. Today is *your* day! Take a vertical leap and watch God move on your behalf.

You are Beautiful!

A PRAYER FOR YOU

Beautiful, I pray your soul be comforted by a mighty King and your wounds healed miraculously. I pray that the Spirit of God breaks every chain of rejection, self-hatred, or abandonment in your life. May the Spirit of wisdom and revelation reveal the heart of the Father that vanishes shame, guilt, insecurity, self-destructive behaviors, and a broken spirit.

May God's sweet whispers of truth affect your heart, dry your tears, pick you up from depression, and restore your joy. Your past is not the end of your story, but the beginning of a beautiful love walk with a King.

Beautiful, may His infallible word cleanse and wash you and may His grace be lavished unsparingly in your life.

May God grant you a love encounter like never before and reveal your beauty through the scars you bear.

In love,

JOZANNE MARIE

DECLARATION OF BRAVERY

Today is a new day
I look not to my circumstances
I walk by faith
I am not too old
I am not too young
To speak.
Break the Silence
I am bold as a lion
My voice will not be caged inside of me
I am brave enough
The Lord has made me brave

Brave to be whole
Brave enough to live in my own skin
Brave to dance to the rhythm of truth
I am brave enough to be a woman
Unique, wise, beautiful
A warrior

I am brave enough to get up after being knocked down
I am brave enough to live past my experience
I will thrive in the sea of impossibilities
I am brave enough to fall into the arms of grace
Laugh at my past
After I have been told I am not worth it.
I am brave enough to accept who God says I am
Hurtful words will not drive me out of my character
Past wounds will not destroy my identity

DECLARATION OF BRAVERY

I will not settle for mediocrity
I will thrive in His Word
Never looking back
I am brave enough
God has made me BRAVE

JOIN THE CAMPAIGN

FOR CENTURIES, LITTLE girls and boys have held in secrets of abuse until they are grown adults. These secrets have caused physical, psychological, and sexual damage to living healthy lives. Join us as we change one community at a time through the BEAUTIFUL CAMPAIGN.

THE BEAUTIFUL CAMPAIGN, in conjunction with *Beautiful*, the play, is created to celebrate, inspire, and create a global movement to free those who have anguished in silence for years over their abuse by awakening voices across the world to release the shame.

To share your story and join the campaign visit: www.jozannemarie.com.

A SPECIAL THANK YOU

IN OUR JOURNEY to *Beautiful,* along the way we encounter people who transform our lives. They take the time to invest in us. They love us even when we don't love ourselves. They share a piece of their own lives with us to help us grow, heal, and prosper. These gems are hard to find and when we discover them, we have no other choice but to cherish them in our hearts. Here are some of the most amazing, brave, gifted, and smart people who took the time to say hello and welcome. You inspire me and I appreciate you all. Life with you in it makes it beautiful.

Thank you…

SUNDAY IDIGA and THE IDIGA FAMILY Thank you, my dear husband, for taking this journey with me. Through the highs and lows, you have been faithful in love, prayer, and faith. Thanks for being my number one cheerleader and best friend. I love you dearly.

Doug Reid, Sydonnie Bown, Senoam McInnis, Doug and Dalia Atchison, Joy and Peter Bohlinger, The Bohlinger Family, Andrea Navedo, Belle Bromfield, Susanna Santiaga, Lisa Fulton, Charlayne Woodard, Marvin Wrightbey, Elle Jai, Leonor Edmondson, Harvey and LaTonya Lewis, Stephanie Whitfield, Francis and Amy Onelum, Bamba and Ganohon Bambadjan, James Price, Christy Lee Hughes, Bryan Kaplan, Marvlyn Harrison, Linda McDill, and Rebecca Okeke.

BEAUTIFUL

A FEW WOMEN WHO INSPIRE ME

Joy Bohlinger: Thanks for being such an amazing mentor and friend. Your love for the broken, your generosity to the orphans, and your kindness to others is an inspiration to many women. It's an honor to walk this life with you.

Kathy Ireland: I remember in high school sitting in my living room, looking at your photo on *Vogue* magazine. Thank you for your grace, humility, and wisdom. You are an inspiration to women worldwide to be leaders of integrity, smart, and to own their beauty. It is such an honor to know you.

Oprah Winfrey: *The Oprah Winfrey Show* has brought me through many dark times. Thanks for sharing your journey with the world and in the midst of it all, a little black girl from Kingston, Jamaica, one day became brave to do the same. Thank you.

Christine Caine: God bless the day you were born, now women no longer have to wear long skirts and huge church hats to give the devil a black eye. Thanks for giving us the permission to be unique and bold.

Maya Angelou: When you made your transition, I wept because although we never met physically, I read every book you have written. I am glad for the day you broke your silence because it allowed millions of women like me to no longer be afraid or ashamed.

Whoopi Goldberg: We stared in each other eyes and smiled, the day I saw your show, *A Funny Thing Happened on the Way to the Forum* on Broadway, right as you were about to enter the limousine. Thanks for inspiring women to be strong, funny, and honest.

A SPECIAL THANK YOU

Viola Davis: I had the privilege to meet you once and like always, you take our breath away. Thank you for inspiring us to be excellent in our craft and always reminding us why God gave us gifts and talent. You are truly an epitome of class and beauty.

In Love,
Jozanne Marie

ABOUT THE AUTHOR

 JOZANNE MARIE IS an acclaimed actress, playwright, poet, speaker, and an advocate for women.

This Jamaican born multi-talented artist is also a NAACP Theatre Awards winner for Best Solo Show: *Beautiful,* which she wrote and performed. *Beautiful* has garnered critical acclaim by various news outlets, magazines and celebrities: Critic's Choice in the *LA Times* and Best of the Week in *Gospel Rhythms Magazine.* This journey led Jozanne to start the National Beautiful Campaign: *The Shame Does Not Belong To You.*

Jozanne is a graduate of the prestigious Acting Studio Conservatory in New York City. She has appeared in Film, TV, and Theatre productions, as well as playing principal roles in many National Commercials, including writing and starring in a **National Campaign for Sprite.**

Her poetry workshop Spit teaches inner city youths to make a difference in their communities by using their own unique voices regarding social issues, such as gang violence, global warming, and sexual assault. Her summer project Men Making a Change was requested and presented to First Lady Michelle Obama.

Jozanne Marie is also an ordained minister. She has served as the president of Tuesday Night Bible Study for Young Adults two years at the West Angeles Church of God in Christ and has performed for some of the largest church communities in her gift of poetry.

Ms. Marie is a member of the Screen Actors Guild, Dramatist Guild, Board Member for the African Artist Association, Co-founder of Sunjoz Productions, and an Associate Programmer for The Bentonville Film Festival which champions women and diverse voices in media.